Labor and Santamaria

Labor and Santamaria

ROBERT MURRAY

Australian Scholarly

First published 2016 by Australian Scholarly Publishing Ltd
7 Lt Lothian St Nth, North Melbourne, Vic 3051
Tel: 03 9329 6963 / Fax: 03 9329 5452
enquiry@scholarly.info / www.scholarly.info

ISBN 978-1-925333-59-6

Cover design by Wayne Saunders

Contents

Abbreviations

ACTU	Australian Council of Trade Unions
ALP	Australian Labor Party
ASIO	Australian Security Intelligence Organisation
AWU	Australian Workers' Union
DLP	Democratic Labor Party
NCC	National Civic Council
QCE	Queensland Central Executive
QLP	Queensland Labor Party
SPA	Socialist Party of Australia
THC	Trades Hall Council
TWU	Transport Workers' Union

Foreword

Midnight to dawn at the old Journalists Club in Phillip Street Sydney in 1954 was a good time and place to follow the origins of the Great Labor Split of 1955. A young Bob Murray and I were able to do just that, in the stimulating atmosphere of Australia's only 24-hour licence in the days of 6 o'clock closing. There was drama aplenty to argue about: the defection of the Soviet diplomat Vladimir Petrov; the 'rescue' of his wife at Darwin airport; the setting up of the Royal Commission on Soviet espionage in Australia; Menzies' survival as Prime Minister against the odds in the 1954 Federal election. There was Dr Evatt's calamitous appearances before the Royal Commission and in October his explosive press statement attacking 'disloyal and subversive' elements inside and outside the Labor Party, particularly in Victoria.

We did not grasp the full implication of these events; and certainly we did not foresee their role in our personal and professional lives. In Bob's case, it began the indispensable contribution he would make to our understanding of them, as the leading historian of the Split.

Until Evatt's Press statement, there was little in the events of 1954 to presage the huge disruption of 1955. To outsiders, Victoria seemed an unlikely target for Evatt's attack. Bob, who did more than any of my newspaper contemporaries to detach my political thinking from a Tory background in Brisbane, was for me something of an authority on Victoria, having been a cadet reporter on the Melbourne *Argus* in the early 1950s. Ironically, in those years it had been it had been the Victorian Liberals who were dysfunctional. In December 1952 John Cain Senior had formed the first majority Labor government; there seemed a fair prospect of years of stable Labor government there.

While the struggle for control of key unions between the ALP-controlled Industrial Groups and the Communist Party figures crucially in any account of the Split, it had been part of the industrial-political landscape in Australia for a decade. Electorally, Labor was enjoying considerable success and held government in every state except South Australia. It had won a slight majority of the vote nation-wide in the 1954 Federal election but lost the election in swinging seats. This tantalising but decisive event unhinged Evatt. One need only read the early parliamentary speeches of the rising newcomer to Canberra, Gough Whitlam, to capture the confidence then pervading Labor, until Evatt's missteps after the election. The element of hubris is unmistakable in the truly Greek tragedy which then unfolded.

The 1955 Split, like its two predecessors, in 1916 over conscription and in 1931 over Depression policies, had an international dimension. The Split was an Australian manifestation of the Cold War. This gave it its deadly power. The sudden collapse of the Soviet Union and the discrediting of communism in 1989–91 has rendered almost incomprehensible many aspects of the Cold War to 21st century generations. Because we avoided a Third World War, inevitably a nuclear war, the ideological threat presented in the Cold War years now tends to be discounted. But it was real; it was not just some invention of senator Joe McCarthy in the United States or of Menzies in Australia. Conservative leaders like the British Prime Minister Harold McMillan were haunted by the failure of liberal capitalism and parliamentary democracy in the 1930s; they genuinely believed that communism might prove a superior economic model. It was easy to dismiss claims that western communist parties were in the pay of Moscow, but they turned out to be true. These parties skilfully exploited the prestige of the Soviet Union based on its massive contribution to the defeat of Nazi Germany.

The Marxist–Leninist analysis of imperialism struck a deep chord in Asia. The Chinese revolution, the Korean War and the French defeat in Indo-China brought the Cold War to Asia in a very hot form. This was profoundly unsettling for a nation which, having fought its war against Japan, was now witnessing the dismantling of the British Empire, the guarantee of its basic doctrine, the White Australia Policy. These were the realities against which the Split was acted out in Australia.

Just as Bob Murray and I could not anticipate the Split, nobody of our generation could foresee the destruction of the Soviet Union and its empire without a Third World War. The outcome of 1989–91 was unimaginable. In 1950, Menzies said that we should prepare for war in three years. The most optimistic predicted a convergence of the two competing systems over time.

While the international aspects gave the Split a wider significance, its essential elements were home grown and very Australian. Its origins lay in the perennial question of the relationship between the Australian Labor Party and the trade unions; its outcome reflected the federal system, with widely different results between the states, especially as between New South Wales and Victoria.

For my own part, however, coming to work for Labor leaders five years after the Split I always found its international aspects the most challenging. In particular, my early years with Arthur Calwell and Gough Whitlam, at least from 1963, were dominated by the Vietnam War. The Labor Left dominated foreign policy. I had the task of articulating Labor policy on Vietnam in an electorally acceptable form. There is no doubt that the absence of the members who had formed the Democratic Labor Party after their expulsion in 1955 made that task easier. Gough Whitlam had a memorable insight into the emotions involved in the issue as early as 1954, after a speech calling for non-intervention in favour of the Geneva Accords; these provided for elections for the whole of Vietnam, which clearly would have been won by the communists. Jack Mullens, the Victorian MP, said: 'That's all very fine Gough but I can't forget that there are three million of my co-religionists who will be slaughtered if the communists take over the south.' It is, I think, a reasonable speculation that the Labor Party would have split over Vietnam if it had not already split in 1955.

As it turned out, a much more divisive issue for Labor was the ancient issue of State Aid for Catholic schools. Opposition to government funding for non-government schools became the test of left-wing orthodoxy. Whitlam's support for the principle of funding for all schools was central to his long struggle to reconstruct the Victorian branch the ALP, the last torrid chapter in the Great Split.

In this book, Bob Murray provides more fascinating insights by examining and reflecting on many of his interviews with most of the principal actors. He proves the truth of the first law of politics: things seldom turn out the way the main actors want, intend or foresee. We set things in motion and then events, usually unforeseen, take over. All politics is about predictions; predictions about human behaviour have an unfortunate habit of being wrong. Politics often seems just one long story of unintended consequences. The Split was no exception. Bob Murray's great achievement has been to make sense of it all.

Graham Freudenberg

Preface

The Split: Australian Labor in the Fifties (Cheshire) first appeared in 1970, when the events of the 1950s were still fresh in memories and most of the participants were still alive. The last reprint (by Hale and Iremonger) was in 1984. Further reprints or editions have been discussed since, but the period was becoming remote for such a large, detailed book.

A simpler, much shorter account seemed appropriate, however, since the founding of the Democratic Labor Party and the career of B.A. Santamaria have remained part of Australian public discussion and have had a continuing impact on public life. The result is *Labor and Santamaria*, which also takes the story into the present century.

It consists partly of newly written chapters, partly of revised versions of material I wrote in the 1990s, and partly of chapters abridged from the original book on, mainly, New South Wales and Queensland.

The spirit of this book does not vary much from the first *Split*, but it does include some additional insights gathered over the years since, especially from informal conversations with people of the time.

Sources for the original *Split* were mainly standard ALP records, earlier histories, about twenty interviews, and the contemporary daily and magazine press. But informal chatting also played quite a role then, as it often does in refining more formal research.

Many books, most listed in the Bibliography, have contributed to my understanding of the era, but three in more recent years have been especially valuable: Bruce Duncan's *Crusade or Conspiracy? Catholics and the Anti-Communist Struggle in Australia* and the two volumes of B.A. Santamaria's papers edited by Patrick Morgan.

I would like to thank Robert Manne for permission to use my contribution on *The Split in The Australian Century* (Text, 1999) and Wayne Saunders for the cover image.

The editions of Colin A. Hughes and B.D. Graham, *A Handbook of Australian Politics and Government* are the source for election results. Chapter 9 is a more informal discussion of sources.

Robert Murray, Melbourne, 2016

Chapter 1

After 'Chif'

A spirit of socialism pervaded Ben Chifley's Labor Party, both in policy and personal principles. In 1947 it had audaciously proposed to nationalise, to bring under government ownership in an enlarged Commonwealth Bank, all the private enterprise banks. The proposal had been defeated in the High Court, but the coldness of public opinion towards it helped bring defeat in 1949. Nevertheless, Labor still believed that many industries should be in government ownership and that governments should plan and control others. It supposed that 'nationalisation' and close government planning of industry would produce a more equal and efficient society – almost the opposite of its beliefs little more than a generation later. However, its socialism was as much to do with its people as its policies. Chifley was one of its few leaders from the ranks of manual workers, though he had had a brief secondary education and worked for a short time as a cashier's assistant in a Bathurst store. He joined the New South Wales Railways as a workshop boy at seventeen. He became a locomotive driver and union activist, punished by railway management for his part in the bitter strike of 1917 until, in 1928, aged forty-three, he won the federal parliamentary seat of Macquarie, which sprawled west from the Blue Mountains. Although a successful political career brought him to the leadership of his country, he remained 'old Chif the engine driver', favouring plain suits and plain hotels near the smells and sounds of railway stations, cups of tea in his semi-detached cottage near the engine whistles and steam smells of Bathurst's ornate old railway station. Many a working man's prejudices remained with him, although his genial warmth, sense, wit, intelligence and apparent sincerity won him friends in business.

Many of the Labor members who sat behind Chifley had similar backgrounds – former railwaymen, ex-shearers and union officials who had risen from workshop floors, and battlers on the land. Those who had the good fortune to be clerks, teachers or lawyers often felt they had to appear 'horny handed', with the occasional dropped 'h' or 'g' in the voice. Labor men (there was only one woman in the federal parliamentary Labor

Party) rarely stayed at the Hotel Canberra, which was plain enough by later standards. They dismissed it as being for 'silvertails' and favoured instead the unadorned Hotel Kurrajong, which served no alcohol, required a walk down the passage in gown and slippers for shower or toilet and was a brisk walk through the sharp Canberra air from Parliament House. It was at the Kurrajong that Chifley suffered his fatal heart attack on 13 June 1951. The night he died, colleagues were dancing at a jubilee ball at Parliament House to mark the opening of a new Liberal-dominated parliament after the voters again rejected Chifley's Labor in the elections of 28 April 1951. It also marked the fifty years since the first commonwealth parliament met.

Even though Chifley was sixty-five when he died, his sudden death left no clear successor and, even less, a path away from the socialism which most of the party loved but the voters rejected. Labor was to drift over the next two decades, torn between the Chifley spirit and its eagerness to return to the government benches, its socialism ebbing away. The splits and feuds which were soon to consume it were not about policy or ideology, but the erosion of the Chifley spirit was the backdrop against which dramas were played out.

The mourners who followed Chifley's cortege out to the Bathurst cemetery in June 1951 included three ambitious, energetic and driven men who aspired to succeed him at Labor's helm. Although all three wanted, almost with desperation, to be prime minister of Australia, none could persuade a majority of colleagues, let alone voters, that they could do the job. The jostling and mistrust between these three was to rock the party for many years. The man caucus chose to succeed Chifley was Dr Herbert Vere Evatt, then aged fifty-six and the most intellectually gifted man in caucus. But, like many intellectually gifted men, he could be blind to what was obvious to others. A brilliant law student whose period at the bar had been brief, he tended to see life through a lawyer's glasses. Evatt had been attorney-general, Minister for External Affairs and deputy prime minister in Chifley's government (1946–49) and that of his wartime predecessor, John Curtin (1941–45). He had a reputation for being, as well as clever, intensely ambitious and in some ways idealistic, even naively so, but also being erratic, and for 'playing the ends against the middle'. Many Labor supporters admired his intellect and his vision for the United Nations; he had been President of the UN General Assembly in 1948–49 and was influential in its founding, but experienced politicians were wary of him.

Evatt's rivals were Arthur Augustus Calwell and Edward John Ward, also successful Labor ministers in the 1940s. Caucus elected Calwell as Evatt's deputy, leaving Ward a frustrated member on the opposition front bench but outside the leadership. Calwell could, in the early 1950s, have been looked on as a figure of the Labor Right in caucus, Ward as representative of its Left, but these labels are of limited value in describing the Labor Party of the day. Calwell was a socialist nationaliser, planner and plain dresser in the Chifley pattern. In his last years in parliament a subtle shift brought him the support of Labor's Marxist left. A strong Catholic, he had earned his right-wing tag in the 1930s through belligerent anti-communism, predominantly expressed in the Victorian branch. Then he was regarded as close to Archbishop Mannix and the sharp tone of his anti-communism, particularly during the Spanish Civil War crisis in the party, reflected that of the Mannix circle. Before entering parliament in 1940 for the safe seat of Melbourne, Calwell had been an accountant in the Victorian State Treasury but, the son of a policeman, he had grown up in working-class West Melbourne. He clung to the Catholicism and Irish sentiments of his mother, who had died when he was sixteen, but could mix easily with people of many backgrounds. He had genial charm and warmth but he could also be vindictive and spiteful. He clung to the Labor Party almost as if it was his family.

'Eddie' Ward was more the Labor fundamentalist and puritan, a good hater, flamboyantly class conscious and strident in his oratorical attacks on the conservatives. In the 1930s he used to say that 'the only good Nat. is a dead one', referring to the Nationals, as the conservatives were known until 1931. He was a militant defence isolationist before World War II and during the war against Japan a bitter opponent of conscription for military service. Hardly a conventional Catholic, he nevertheless read the Bible regularly as part of life-long self-education in the classics. Many Australians admired him as the parliamentary representative of the militant working man. As with Chifley, Ward and Calwell impressed many – but far from all – Australians as 'sincere' or 'good Labor men'. A later generation might have thought them 'authentic'

Rather than a Marxist, as some left-wingers were, Ward was the chief representative in caucus of those who had looked to Jack Lang for inspiration, the New South Wales Labor leader from 1923 to 1939. By the 1950s, although Lang was largely a discredited old man, the extraordinary passions he could arouse in his home state and party continued to be a wild-card in the Labor pack. The point about Lang was not so much one of policy as of a cast of mind – many critics saw in him an unsuccessful Australian reflection of the fascist leaders of Europe, though the comparison is far-fetched. Nevertheless, the suspicion remained strong that 'Langism' was a contagion, politically treacherous, intimidating and demagogic, looking to mob oratory as its tool. Ward, then a young Sydney tramways clerk and boxer, had entered parliament in 1931 as a pro-Lang candidate during a period of division over the Great Depression. He largely rehabilitated himself and became Minister for Labour and National Service (1941–43) and Transport and External Territories (1943–49).

Labor's real problems were not so much in parliament, where internal divisions and lack of outstanding talent are common enough, but in its complex and far-flung organisational wing. In the 1950s this was based on the trade unions much more than it would be a generation later. Up to 80 per cent of delegates to the party's state conferences, its main centres of power, came from affiliated trade unions. There had always been left and right strands in the unions, as among the Labor parliamentarians, but a brilliantly organised campaign in the late 1930s had brought many of the unions under the control of the Communist Party. In the eyes of many Australians World War I and the savage economic depression that followed in the early 1930s, with another war coming a few years later, left western capitalist democracy discredited. This explained the wide appeal of socialist solutions, whether Chifley-style through the Labor Party or through revolutionary communism.

In the 1940s the Communist Party believed that in the Soviet Union and the rule of Josef Stalin lay the solution to the world's problems. Tightly organised on military lines and fanatical in their belief, by the 1940s the 'commos' wielded ruthless influence in the trade unions – where the depression had sapped the morale of the older generation of leaders and undermined their members' confidence in them. By 1945, the Communist Party controlled at least a third of the votes at the Australian Council of Trade Unions (ACTU) Congress and got enough support from the Labor left and independents for a motion to increase the power of the ACTU at the expense of state and local trades halls. Yet this would be the communist high noon. From that point communist influence in the unions slipped away. This was partly because of the increasing dislike of the Soviet Union among Australians and partly because of a declining faith in the cause by communists themselves.

In the critical decade after the war, the ALP and the moderate unions effectively took the fight back to the communists. The main weapon was the ALP Industrial Groups. The ALP, through decisions of most of its state conferences after 1945, endorsed and supported, with money and organisation, groups of union members fighting to win back unions from the Communist Party. It was a vital campaign for the ALP. Though communist strategy, laid down from Moscow, varied from time to time, in the postwar period the communists fought Labor as a rival party. They withdrew unions

Communist union officials had a bitter political hatred of ALP Industrial Groups and others who opposed them in the battles of the 1940s and 50s for control of the Australian union movement. To be against them was to be an insidious traitor to the working class. This cartoon is from *Labor News*, organ of the Federated Ironworkers Association, centre of the biggest battles for election to union positions. In practice both the communists and groupers produced many popular union officials, often more dedicated than older style moderates, but the 'commos' also lost support because they called frequent strikes.

McClintock, *Labor News*, May 1949

The National Herb-Evarium

Federal Labor Leader H.V. Evatt soon had trouble on his hands with the New South Wales and Victorian branches of the ALP over his press statement on 5 October 1954 attacking the groupers, whose supporters dominated the two biggest branches of the Party.

Wep, *Daily Telegraph*, 24 October 1954

they controlled from affiliation – thus depriving the ALP of revenue; they often sought to embarrass Labor politically with strikes and hostile propaganda. The frequent strikes, especially in transport and coal and the general atmosphere of conflict, disruption and economic damage angered the public. The conservative parties tried to portray Labor as influenced by, or weak towards, the communists. This was another compelling reason for Labor to fight back. The Industrial Groups were highly successful, checking the communists from increasing their strength after 1945 and, in dramatic battles, winning some big unions back to Labor. The most notable were the Federated Ironworkers' Association and the Federated Clerks' Union. With these unions, victory came only after the groupers successfully claimed in the courts that the communists had rigged the ballots.

For the first few years, the Groups were uncontroversial, their work too essential and appreciated by all but the far left of the ALP. As the communist tide receded, however, one particular aspect turned ALP opinion against the Groups. This was the inside role that the Catholic Church and its clandestine organisational arm, the Catholic Social Studies Movement, better known – if known at all – as 'the Movement' played.

The Movement comprised Catholic laymen directed through the official Catholic Action office in Melbourne. It had followers organised in unions and small parish groups over much of Australia, ready to support the ALP Industrial Groups. It prepared lists of Catholic unionists who could be canvassed in union elections and provided clerical, transport and sometimes monetary assistance during union elections.*

The Catholic Church was one of the main anti-communist forces internationally and the Movement reflected this. It had several peculiar features, however, which within a few years destroyed it in its original form. One of these was the ambition of its visionary and lucid leader, Bartholomew Augustine Michael ('Bob') Santamaria. A prodigious writer and commentator on affairs from the 1930s to the 1990s, capable of being both astonishingly perceptive and wrong-headed, Santamaria built the Movement into a political weapon in its own right. Members joined political parties, mainly Labor, supported pro-Group and anti-communist policies there and encouraged anti-communist opinion generally. The Movement favoured some domestic policies which won it few friends, such as closer settlement, particularly of immigrants, on the land and greater co-operation between unions and employers. However, its main cause politically was a strongly anti-communist foreign policy, which was not an easy fit for a Labor Party

* The ALP Industrial Groups controlled by the Party and the Movement were quite separate organisations that collaborated. Typically about a third of Group members were also Movement people, but this was not often a difficulty at the industrial level.

inclined against military commitment. Santamaria cultivated the Catholic priesthood, brothers and nuns, particularly trainees, and by the early 1950s many were militant supporters, often preaching Movement views from the pulpit. As well as the theoretical magazine *Twentieth Century*, the Movement published the lively *News Weekly*, which had the same pugnacious, agitating style as the communist weeklies, *Tribune* and *Guardian*.

The Movement and Industrial Groups became increasingly embroiled in Labor factional politics. The ALP had long displayed a tendency to split into right and left wings, though the dividing issues varied and were more likely to be questions of emphasis rather than deep fissures. From the 1940s to the 1960s, however, the Communist Party dominated the militant section, through its own disciplined members as officials in alliance with people prepared to work with it for various, typically as much industrial as political, reasons. The 'commos' were often good, dedicated union officials.

The biggest division over the Industrial Groups in the early 1950s was whether they should have a national organisation or be officially confined, as they had been, to one-state organisations. An ambition to disband them also emerged in the early 1950s once the worst of the communist challenge was over.

Some socialists were sympathetic to the communists and the young 'socialist' societies of Europe and Asia, although outright admiration for the Soviet Union or for the Communist Party's muscular methods was not so common. There was often a sneaking sympathy for the communists as dedicated battlers for the working class, especially once their wings in the unions had been clipped. While this view was common enough at the local and shop-floor level, experienced politicians understood the differences between the goals and methods of Labor and the Communist Party.

Several factors gave the anti-Group campaign the momentum to take it towards the centre of Labor affairs. One was simple factionalism. Group supporters by 1952 controlled the party in the three biggest states in an alliance with moderate unions and sympathetic parliamentarians. In these states the controlling line-up was a coalition of older moderate union leaders and unions won back to the ALP by the Group successes and the Movement. This coalition had made enemies and created rivals in securing its position, but the division was as much 'ins' and 'outs' as about policy. The Groups had never existed in Western Australia and Tasmania, and in South Australia the state conference disbanded them in 1951. In these three states, communist influence was much weaker than in New South Wales, Victoria and Queensland. The tendency there was to keep out potentially disruptive interstate trends. These smaller states became the power-base of the federal secretary of the ALP, Victorian senator, from 1953, Patrick John Kennelly, a fervent Chifleyite who had fallen out with the grouper faction in his own state.

With a stammer he learned to use with theatrical effect, a dry, biting wit and legendarily wily backroom organizing ability, 'Pat' was a memorable ALP figure. His trouble was that many thought him what would later be called a 'control freak', out to control the Party, especially the super-sensitive pre-selections for parliamentary candidates. He in turn thought the groupers to be fanatical and risked a split in the Party. The feud became deeply personal and saw Kennelly lose the Victorian Secretary position in 1950 and his pre-selection for the Legislative Council in 1952, but win a Senate seat in 1953.

The Movement was active in this drama and made many enemies through flamboyant attacks on Kennelly and his faction, and its continued brash intervention in ALP factions led, in 1951, to the federal executive proscribing its *News Weekly* as 'anti-Labor'. Each Sunday Movement people sold *News Weekly* outside many of Australia's Catholic churches.

In the background also was a growing suspicion in the general community of what was called Catholic Action. The bishops had set up the Australian National Secretariat of Catholic Action in 1937 to oversee several lay organisations, in accordance with Vatican policy. The official organisations were controversial, if at all, because critics believed them ineffectual or inappropriately run. Since its inception, however, more sensitive Protestants had looked on Catholic Action as an organ for aggressive Vatican intervention in Australian affairs. In practice the Movement was the only body under Catholic Action supervision to be of much influence and its brief was limited to combating communism. But because it worked in secrecy without a real name, it was poorly understood and an aura of sinister mystique surrounded Catholic Action. The communists, with a flair for identifying and discrediting their enemies, freely labelled opponents as Catholic Actionists, catching not a few Protestants in the net. At the popular level, Catholic Action tended to become a code name suggesting militant, extremist Catholicism.

The Movement also lost friends through its support of the Communist Party Dissolution Bill, the measure by which Prime Minister Robert Menzies proposed to ban the Communist Party and make it illegal for communists to hold trade union office. Labor generally opposed this as a draconian blow at civil liberties. The Movement supported it because Santamaria took the view that the Cold War between the Soviet bloc and the west would turn 'hot', with Australian communists throwing their union power behind the Soviet Union. While this was the extreme view, there was a widespread fear in the last, maddest years of Stalin's life that a shooting war could start. Korea, where war had raged from 1950, was one potential location for wider conflict; isolated Berlin another. The Middle East was also a possible spot for Australian involvement because of economic dependence on the Suez Canal.

Whatever the international fears, outside the Movement the proposed ban on the Communist Party had minimal ALP support. Yet more right-wing sections wanted Labor to let the bill through the Senate, where until 1951 it had a majority. Menzies was looking for an opportunity to dissolve both houses of parliament so he could win control of the Senate. Labor right-wingers argued that an election fought on communism could lose Labor more seats, while if the bill was passed Menzies would find the ban difficult and embarrassing to implement. There was a belief that Menzies himself did not want the bill passed but saw it as a way of embarrassing Labor. The 1948 Queensland conference of the Country Party originally sought the ban and it became coalition policy. After much wrangling, Labor decided by a small majority to let the bill pass in October 1950. Opposition to the ban had been a heartfelt cause for Chifley and the right-wing resistance to his wish in his last months was not forgotten.

Menzies finally secured a double dissolution of the parliament because Labor would not pass a government bill to place a board rather than a governor in charge of the Commonwealth Bank. Close Canberra control over central banking was a key issue for Chifley and the further reluctance of the Labor right to risk a double dissolution had made them unpopular with the party orthodox. There had also been heated left–right Labor divisions over Menzies' legislation allowing the arbitration court (predecessor of Fair Work Australia) to control union elections under certain conditions. But when both of these measures became law, unlike the communist ban they soon ceased to be controversial. Critics by then were privately accusing Chifley of becoming rigid and dogmatic.

The 1951 parliamentary battles over banking and arbitration changes and the Communist Party Dissolution Act had been part of what the Melbourne *Age* on 15 March called 'the most acute public tension in Canberra's history'. During this period the Menzies-controlled House of Representatives sent bills to the Senate which the government knew would embarrass and divide Labor, on both anti-communist grounds and the fears of members in swinging seats. None knew then that these were the last weeks of Chifley's life, but the hurt he felt from division in the party over what he considered major principles was long remembered.

Communist Party publicity in the postwar era, which was modelled on that of the Soviet Union, was strident, exaggerated and doctrinaire. This 1950 leaflet appeared during Prime Minister Robert Menzies' attempt to ban the Communist Party

The 18 April double dissolution election, in the event, turned more on economic issues. Labor won five seats, though Menzies won control of the Senate. With Chifley dead six weeks after the election the anti-communist measure became an immediate test of Evatt's leadership, as Menzies secured a referendum on a proposal to add to the Constitution provision for the Commonwealth to make laws about communism. The previous year, at the peak of caucus sensitivity over the potential electoral damage through the bill, Evatt had accepted a brief from the communist-led Waterside Workers' Federation to oppose the ban in the High Court. After a long hearing the court found the ban to be unconstitutional. Evatt had not consulted caucus about his appearance. There was obvious ground for sensitivity about how Labor would approach the referendum, but the federal executive, still dominated by Chifleyites, moved in before there was any argument and ordered a 'No' campaign. Evatt then led Labor in an energetic campaign which, in September 1951, brought defeat of the Menzies proposals by a small majority. After two excitable and divisive years little more was then heard of the communist ban. Evatt's success won him enduring status in the Labor movement, especially on the Left. Even on the Right, however, he retained warm support.

Evatt's obvious strategy in the three years before an election was due in 1954 was to say as little as possible about socialism and nationalisation, to encourage the 'Catholic vote' and to maintain the attack on Menzies, whom he hated. About two-thirds of Catholics voted Labor in the postwar years, preferring the less imperial, more working-class of the two main party groupings and about 60 per cent of the federal Labor parliamentarians were Catholics, at least nominally. As a group Catholics were slightly more working-class than Protestants, but middle-class, rural and wealthy Catholics were more likely to vote Labor than Protestant equivalents. The propensity of Catholics to vote Labor was a critical factor in keeping the Labor vote up towards 50 per cent of the electorate, despite the unpopularity of its socialism.

Having won the Left with his defeat of the communist ban, Evatt set out to cultivate the groupers, with their appeal to more conservative Catholics. He formed an alliance with the ALP Victorian branch where the secretary was Denis Lovegrove, an intensely anti-communist ex-communist, (who had defeated Kennelly for the job) and his assistant, Frank McManus. Lovegrove was the official leader of the Groups in Victoria and McManus was active in the Movement. Evatt personally cultivated right-wing Victorian MPs such as Stan Keon, who most reflected Movement thinking in caucus, and the independent-minded Bill Bourke. Evatt's firm support for the groupers alienated the centre element around the federal secretary, Kennelly, who had been Chifley's favourite, but that would only be a problem if Labor lost in 1954. Evatt's tilt to the Right resulted in widening the gap between his ambitious deputy, Calwell, and the younger Catholic right elements in Victoria; Calwell had never liked the Movement.

The half-Senate election of 9 May 1953 brought an encouraging result for Evatt. Labor polled 50.6 per cent of the vote, the coalition only 44.4 per cent. (In 1951 Labor polled 47.6 per cent and the coalition 50.3 per cent.) While there was an element of by-election protest about a half-Senate election, the result clearly suggested Labor should hold to its course and perhaps produce a sweetening surprise at election time in 1954.

The economic issue on which Evatt concentrated after the anti-communist referendum was the 'stop-go' propensity of the economy, with inflation and excessive imports impeding economic growth. Postwar inflation had surged with the boom in wool prices in the Korean War and imports flooded in as the postwar world returned to its full productive capacity. This led to the Menzies government calling a squeeze on bank credit in 1951, which produced a recession in 1952 and an unemployment rate of 4 per cent for several months. This was a minute slump by 1930s standards but high for the war and postwar years, and unnerving for a community with strong memories of the depression. Yet there was little, in reality, that Labor could do about the economy. The most divisive issue of the time was to do with foreign affairs.

The foreign policy challenge in the 1950s came not from faraway Moscow but from Peking. The Communist Party under Mao Zedong had won control of China by the gun in 1949. The Chinese People's Republic was a baffling development for Australians. Were its controllers rural reformers or minions of Moscow? Would they seek to export their revolution beyond the Chinese borders? Would they direct their vast army south, as they did in Korea in 1950? Theories abounded but nobody knew the reality. China had been a society effectively closed to the world for decades and was now undergoing momentous change.

Before the war Labor had looked forward to an Asia dominated by democratic socialism, freed of colonial rule. Chifley's model Asian society was Pandit Nehru's India. Many Labor people hoped China would go the same way. Labor tended to see most problems as stemming from unequal distribution of wealth and vividly contrasted the wealth of Indian rajahs, the comfortable life of colonial officials and the reported corruption of the Chinese Nationalists, with the gruelling poverty of most Asians. The

Cold War was difficult for Labor, with its historic attraction to defence isolationism, even pacifism, and ingrained mistrust of big western, imperial powers, 'Wall Street' and 'the Pentagon', Asian 'planters' and similar bogies. Unlike the conservative side, it had never been comfortable with British or other 'colonialists'.

There was no practical alternative, however, to the Cold War alliance with the US and Britain, which had to be maintained by custom, with Australia the weakest partner. Many Labor supporters and most other Australians now feared a large and powerful China. The Movement adopted as dogma the most anti-communist of possibilities. This was the 'threat from the north' – that China would foment and tightly control, in association with Moscow, revolution in the poverty-stricken nations to the south. The urgent, alarming threat from the Moscow-Peking axis, as it was often called, became the Movement's dominating call, as expressed with inimitable stridency in *News Weekly* over the following years. Stan Keon, the MP for Yarra and the Labor member most representative of the Movement, at one point called for almost a 'preventive war', as did more extreme anti-communists in the US.

There was, nevertheless, something in the 'threat from the north' theory. In Vietnam communists controlled the nationalist movement seeking Indo-Chinese independence from France. Malaya, Indonesia and the Philippines all had strong, disciplined communist parties accepting direction from the Kremlin. These societies were emerging from colonial rule; all were poor and their stability was suspect. A more moderate view than the Movement's would have been more sceptical about the likelihood of communists winning everywhere, given the strength of Islam in Malaysia and Indonesia and of Catholicism in the Philippines. It would also have pointed out the difficulty of invading Australia, while being aware of the dangers ideologically hostile neighbours could present – such as the fomenting revolution in New Guinea.

In retrospect the Cold War could be seen as winding down after Stalin's death in 1953. But it would take an astute and lucky seer to have predicted this at the time. The great symbolic issue became whether Australia should diplomatically recognise 'Red' China. The Menzies government sided with the US in continuing to recognise the Nationalist Chinese remnants in Taiwan as the true government of China. Labor sentiment was to recognise the communist government in Peking, as Britain had. The end of the Korean War in mid-1953 increased pressure for 'settlement' of the recognition question and China's admission to the United Nations.

Aware of the need for right-wing Catholic butter for his electoral bread, Evatt's response to the potentially divisive question of recognising China in the lead-up to the elections of 1953 and 1954 was to say as little as possible about it. As Peking was then in a deeply isolationist phase, diplomatic recognition by Australia in the 1950s would have been more likely to antagonise the US, which recognised the Taiwan anti-communist government, than achieve much. But it remained symbolic.

Chapter 2

The ALP

State conference is the heart of the Australian Labor Party. Hundreds of the – more or less – faithful gather to debate and decide policy and rules and to hear, amid thunderous applause, thumping speeches from the federal and state leaders. Conference decides the rules under which MPs will be pre-selected, chooses the State Executive to rule the organisation for the year and elects delegates to the more distant federal executive and conference, which in contestable theory have supreme power. Delegates to the conference come from both the affiliated unions and from electoral councils chosen by the local branches in each state electorate. Many of the big political names of the day are there, but as visitors or as delegates from unions or local electoral councils, not in their own right. Dozens of agenda items come in from branches and unions for debate and, hopefully, be decided as policy, though they are more likely to be neglected than even rejected.

There is – or should be – a lot of raw democracy at work. Sometimes it is clear in the spirited, often angry clashes on conference floor. At other times private caucuses or even more private gatherings will have decided sensitive issues in advance and often 'disciplined' their team to all vote accordingly – or else be very unpopular. Sometimes the great questions of the world are aired, but more often the adage 'all politics is local' is at work: union and municipal council elections, disputes over pre-selection of candidates for parliament, demands for particular action from a Labor State Government or a local council. A seemingly arcane change of rules or procedure can have important consequences for those involved. Controversial agenda items are likely to be among the majority of items that never make it to conference floor, since even a long weekend conference cannot get through all those submitted and printed on the agenda – and the agenda committee knows its job. For the initiated it is all fascinating; for nearly everybody else mind-numbing.

Labor has more of both virtues and vices than the cooler conservatives. It yearns more for conspicuous progress. True Laborites really love the party.

The socialist spirit of 'solidarity' is proclaimed, but more often than not is difficult to achieve. A touch of romance about the Party and its mission is common. Ordinary Labor voters, outside the charmed circle of members and insiders, usually expect less, but they like the tribal pride of feeling that the working man's team could govern as well, or better, than the middle class parties. They also look to Labor to soften the sharp edges of the economy more than the conservatives would.

Conference delegates are likely to include a few rogues, cranks and control freaks, many more passionate 'true believers' in the Labor cause, obsessives, naive idealists, people ambitious (sometimes vaultingly so and planning shrewdly) to become future MPs. It is not unknown for some people to combine all these qualities. Gossip is incessant, swapped about personalities and the politics of the day. It can be one of the main attractions for attending, though usually confined to the corridors and nearby hostelries. In off-stage chatting, some delegates might be discussed as future ministers or leaders – or ridiculed as too obviously aspiring to future greatness. An almost religious fervour for the cause readily coexists with witty cynicism. The Labor Movement has its own jargon and delegates have to know it to be effective. Labor politics can be as much about how you say it as what you say. It is a commonplace for Laborites to suppose that people who do not support Labor, unless it is in their economic interest to vote for the coalition, have been misled by snobbery or by the press. The Labor lawyers are a distinctive, prestigious breed, better educated and paid than most, mostly attached to law firms identified with particular union groupings.

In the 1950s the conferences were rowdier, beerier, smokier and more relentlessly blue-collar than half a century later. They were more of an assertive jamboree for the lesser paid, mostly less powerful half of Australian society, expressing its pride and resentment. Union officials more often than decades later had worked in the trade or industry concerned and remained close to the working members. Delegates were far less likely to be well-educated professional officials, in an age when the Intermediate Certificate at about secondary year four was considered a fair education. Probably a third or even half of delegates would have served in one or another of the two great world wars. Except in Queensland, conference was usually held at the capital city, in the trades hall or perhaps a town hall. New South Wales met in the Sydney town hall.

The unions sent between two-thirds and eighty per cent of the delegates to conference, compared with fifty per cent in the early 21st century. There were more unions, smaller and more specialised and most affiliated with the ALP. Few in the Labor mainstream then were 'white-collar'. Smaller unions were likely to be based on specific crafts such as boiler-making, blacksmithing or roof tiling. The private caucus rooms at conference were much more smoke-filled, more beer flowed in more pubs amid more tobacco ash. Meals were more likely to be Anglo-Celtic meat and 'vegies' in pub counter lunches and hotel dining rooms, rather than Chinese. Delegates usually dressed in collar and tie, perhaps with a sports coat and slacks; workers who wore overalls all week liked to dress up for outings. Those aged over about 30 and many younger would be wearing felt hats. Women were a small minority, but often influential both as wives, daughters and secretaries and through women's organising councils and the like. Labor often ran in families over several generations, with discernible 'dynasties'. And it was still, if fading, the practice for the 50s delegates, as with members of the humblest local branch, to call each other by the old socialist 'comrade' or 'brother'.

Usual practice was and is for unions to affiliate to the party on membership numbers; the more its members the more money it subscribed to the Party, but also the more delegates it could send to conference. In the postwar years the biggest union in most states was the Australian Workers' Union, which mainly represented rural workers, but also some non-coal miners. Shearers, shed hands, farm workers and cane cutters formed the base membership and its conference delegates often had discernible rustic ways. The far-flung and often itinerant and uninterested, if not unenthusiastic, nature of the AWU membership gave it the reputation of being a 'union of officials, for officials, by officials'. Its paid organisers were reputedly large men, tough enough scrappers to ensure that recalcitrant seasonal workers paid their dues. Other unions usually disliked it, as the wide AWU brief facilitated rivalry for members and job coverage. The dominating AWU official in the 1950s and 1960s was 'big Tom' Dougherty, the General (National) Secretary, a large, domineering Queenslander who moved to Sydney to take the top job and liked to exert his substantial muscle in the ALP.

Dougherty's writ ran firmly in the eastern States. His great internal rival was the Adelaide Labor MP Clyde Cameron, who had been an AWU official before entering the Commonwealth Parliament in 1949. Through family and other connections, he was able to control the South Australian branch. In Cameron's acerbic view, Dougherty was corrupt and a 'boss's man' who did not service his members satisfactorily. That did not stop them from being temporary allies in the Split period, though Cameron's union numbers and his close association with the ALP State Secretary in SA, Jim Toohey, enabled him to be a dominant influence in his home state Labor, especially on national questions. Dougherty met his match again in Western

Australia in another authoritarian, Frederick Edward 'Joe' Chamberlain, who doubled up as Secretary of the WA Unions Industrial Council and State secretary of the ALP. Dour and stubborn, Chamberlain was a masterly desk politician, who knew how to assemble and control union votes. His desk and arbitration skills made him popular with unionists, but he was not always so popular with the politicians. A young English immigrant of the 1920s, Chamberlain had begun his political career organising angry farmers wanting redress for a troubled immigrant farm development scheme. He then got his foot on the rungs of the Labor ladder as a Perth tramway worker. In both Adelaide and Perth, the main tendency was to keep interstate troubles at bay; it required a deft balancing act. Most union national offices were in Sydney or Melbourne. Federal Conference and Federal Executive then comprised six and two delegates respectively from each state, irrespective of population, so that Cameron and Chamberlain were key figures nationally.

Big delegations at state conferences came also from unions representing railway and other public transport workers, miners, iron and steel, building, textile, clothing, automotive and waterside workers. Craft-based and smaller unions often banded together to counter the power of the big unions. Industrial issues, great and small, greatly influenced conference; for most delegates union activity was a years-old career and livelihood. A visitor could be excused for thinking that most delegates seemed more interested in union affairs than more political ones. Paid officials and unpaid job delegates filled most of the union delegations, but often Labor Party enthusiasts, some of them ambitious for a seat in parliament, helped fill out otherwise partly empty ranks as proxies.

Most unions at state conferences were regarded as 'moderate', until the Communist Party returned after 1952 to reaffiliating unions it controlled. This process was still underway in the mid-50s. As members of a rival party, Communist Party members could not attend conference, but that Party exerted influence through cooperative ALP members manning its delegations. These built up the Marxist-oriented left wing of conference. A right wing came from unions the ALP-endorsed Industrial Groups had wrested from communist control. The Clerks and, especially in New South Wales, Ironworkers were the two biggest of these. While most moderate union officials strongly opposed Communist Party influence in their own ranks, they looked with awe on the new, often brash and young groupers. Paid fulltime officials rarely wanted to go back to the factory floor and felt uneasy about a political machine which could topple once over-weening union leaders.

Labor memories are famously long and the past exerted a huge influence on conference delegates. In the 50s, memories readily went back to World War I and the conscription and other boiling issues of those days. Recollection of the 1930s depression and World War II were even keener. Off-stage, delegates swapped tales of hardship and of the perfidy of various wrangling politicians of the hard depression times, when wages fell and most politicians (and many union officials) lost their jobs. Tough times while growing up have ever been a valuable asset in Labor politics.

In NSW, the air was still brittle in the 50s with the memory of the divisive depression-era Premier, Jack Lang. With his bombast and thundering denunciations Lang had at least been able to dramatize the fate of the unemployed and propose ways to combat the slump, even if they were unworkable. In the 1950s, the old drama queen still exerted an unsettling influence from the side-lines with his weekly *Century* magazine, which specialised in diatribes and witty snipes at ALP politicians. World War II was a cause for Labor pride, through the leadership of ALP Prime Minister from 1941–45, John Curtin. For some, it was an after-event conversion, since ALP figures had been prominent 'appeasers' of Nazi Germany in the dramatic lead-up to the war and some had bitterly opposed Curtin's wartime policy of conscripting men for military service.

To back up their debating points, delegates would readily invoke the memory of Curtin, Chifley and Jim Scullin, who was Prime Minister from 1929–31 but whose Government split over depression economic policy and finally fell when a third faction crossed the floor. Delegates did not always remember that the final blow against Scullin came from a Lang-oriented group from NSW, not 'the banks' or 'money men', as many believed. The feuding in NSW Labor in the 1920s and 1930s had become so drawn-out and complicated that few then or later could easily explain its origins.

The ALP felt itself to be surrounded by enemies, in the Liberal and Country parties, the press, the banks and big business generally and perhaps the security services. The great satan for any Labor gathering, at least publicly, was Prime Minister Robert Menzies. Little would get more cheers from conference than a slashing, sneering speech attacking 'Mr Menzies'. Menzies was felt to be governing superciliously for the better-off half of the community, against those Labor represented. A non-Labor Premier would also get his share of diatribes, but State government was a problem, since Labor ruled in many states and was therefore often the biggest employer. Delegates would normally be circumspect in public, but privately critical of employment and other government policies. Unions might hope to get favourable legislation from Labor governments on issues like worker's compensation, job safety and conditions and there was always the lure of a government appointment or seat in parliament, but as ever the limitations of the public purse kept a frustratingly tight rein on government action. Many unionists wondered off-stage whether Labor and its governments were worth the cost of affiliation. Corruption was always a worry, though discussed off-stage rather than on. Some Labor-controlled inner city local councils were notorious for it. State governments were not generally corrupt, but one or two ministers, some officials or a particular controversial deal or misguided policy might be. No state was exempt, though NSW and Queensland were the usual suspects.

The rival Communist Party got its share of loud condemnation from the floor as well. The peak year was 1948, the memorable year of the 'red baiters' picnic' at the Victorian Conference. This was the time when the Communist Party almost had the strength, through the unions it dominated, to control the Trades Hall Council and the ACTU. Internationally it was the hottest time of the Cold War, with a Communist coup in Czechoslovakia and a Communist army about to march on Peking to claim China. Back in Australia, the ALP Industrial Groups were waging their battle to win communist-controlled unions back to the ALP. However, over the next few years ALP observers began to note a cooling of conference support for the groupers when they overturned the communists in several big unions.

The ALP was officially 'socialist' but few knew what that really meant. The official platform committed it to 'socialisation of the means of production and exchange'. Most Labor people would reluctantly concede that it did not mean nationalising much more industry but they were not so good at explaining what it did mean. 'Social democracy' and 'democratic socialism' were two favourite alternatives to 'socialism' as shorthand descriptions for ALP policy. 'Social justice' was another favoured aim. In practice, all these boiled down to support for the existing 'mixed economy' of mostly commercial enterprises plus a few big basic industries in government hands; but Laborites might advocate as well a bit more nationalisation, economic planning and taxing of the rich to help the poor. A socialist theorist at conference seeking more precise definitions from delegates would probably encounter a lot of blank stares. The same would happen to a delegate trying to pin colleagues down on the practical or budgetary problems of more ambitious welfare or national development proposals. Labor was happiest talking about itself – and its enemies.

The most notable Labor Premier of the '50s was John Joseph 'Joe' Cahill, of NSW, shrewd, competent, calm, conspicuously unostentatious. Lang's

Century called him 'old smoothie'. In his plain blue double breasted blue seats and maroon ties, slightly mangled speech (he would say 'tremenjous' instead of tremendous), Cahill presented as the typical 'plain man' of his era (born 1891) and former railway fitter. But he had the political guile to successfully guide a tempestuous party organisation away from the wracked memories of the '30s and through the next damaging split that came in the mid-50s. And though he was personally a brass band lover, the Sydney Opera House was Joe Cahill's vision and he induced a grudging party to support it.

In Victoria, another avuncular, 'plain man' in pipe-puffing John Cain was premier from 1952 until his Government split in 1955. Cain had led the Party since 1935, gruelling years with only two short periods of office until 1952. Victorian Labor had historically been weakened by the distribution of seats in the State Parliament. Dating back to colonial times, this almost eccentrically favoured the otherwise fairly small Country (later National party) because of the small number of voters required for rural as compared to city seats. The imbalance allowed the Country Party to play both bigger parties off against each other to hold office as a minority government, which it did especially between 1935–45 and again during 1950–52. For most of this time, Labor sitting on the cross-benches had kept the Country Party in office in return for fairly small concessions.

Cain's early 1950s government was the first in which Labor had ever held a majority in its own right. It had its problems and tensions, but was governing fairly well until the crisis hit. Unlike its counter-parts in NSW and Queensland, Victorian Labor had a relatively small AWU and mining industry, bastions of Labor voters in most states. Cain's closest, but also most controversial, colleague was the legendary P.J. (Pat) Kennelly, a dedicated, if somewhat authoritarian and controlling 'Labor man' who combined charm and a wicked wit with a famous stammer. Kennelly had started in the ALP office as a young clerk in 1926, became State Secretary from 1946–49, Federal Secretary from 1946–54, a Member of the Legislative Council from 1938–52, a senator from 1953–67. He was Labor's Deputy Leader in the Senate from 1956–67. One of a state or federal secretary's jobs was to raise enough money from outside sources to subsidise the union and local branch contributions in running the party organsiation and at elections. Pat Kennelly was personally austere, but considered a master in winning contributions from business.

The Queensland Premier from 1952 to 1957 was Vincent Gair, a one-time railway clerk, jaunty, tubby, and like many Queensland premiers somewhat authoritarian in his ways. The party met only every three years, as the Labor in Politics Conference, held in a different city each time. The AWU usually expected to dominate there, but was increasingly being challenged by the more left-wing or Industrial Group unions of the Brisbane and regional trades halls. There was also a potential problem in the longstanding personal dislike between Gair and Rochus Joseph John ('Joe') Bukowski, the AWU state 'boss' and a Tom Dougherty protégé.

Tasmania was another state where Labor was often in office, backed by the AWU. The ageing Sir Robert Cosgrove, Premier from 1939–58, was one of the very few Labor men ever to accept a knighthood. His deputy and successor, Eric Reece was a former AWU organiser. Governments changed more often in Western Australia, where Bert Hawke was Labor Premier from 1953–59. Another in the unostentatious 'plain man' pattern, Hawke was an uncle of, and inspiration to, Bob Hawke, Prime Minister from 1983–91. South Australia was barren ground for Labor at state level. Another plain man, former orchardist Tom Playford, was a conservative Premier from 1938–65, helped by a favourable distribution of seats and a wily talent for governing well. A more promising new Labor generation entering the Parliamentary Party was typified by Don Dunstan, later Premier 1967–68 and 1970–79. A dapper lawyer, Dunstan won a seat in 1953.

In principle the parliamentary parties these men and the Federal leader, Dr Evatt, led were as much representatives of the ALP organisation as of the voters who elected the members to parliaments. The organisational wing, with its union domination, was perceived as directly representative of the workers. Old-time socialist lore was that fighters for the workers became 'soft' and cautious once in parliament. Tension between the 'industrial' and 'political' wings was common, especially when Labor was in government and it was prudent political management to keep it to a minimum and out of the public eye.

The rules for 'pre-selecting' intending parliamentary candidates for Labor endorsement varied between states. In NSW members of local party branches within the electorate concerned voted to choose their candidate. In Victoria, members of affiliated unions living in the electorate could vote as well. It was common practice for MPs and people with political ambitions to encourage friends, relations and allies to join the party, in order to increase or protect their prospects, but more rampant 'branch stacking' was not so common.

Labor seemed to govern at is best in the states. The Commonwealth Labor governments had either split, as in World War I, or adopted and then handled badly extravagant policies, such as bank nationalisation in 1947–9. The 1929–31 Scullin Government both dabbled unsuccessfully in ultra-controversial policy, such as repudiating payments due on loans and creating credit; and it then split over a separate issue. State Labor governments, by contrast, were generally as successful as those of the conservatives, given the myriad difficulties – and some temptations – of providing state services on limited budgets. This was an odd contrast with traditional Labor policy, which verged on hallowed dogma, of wanting states abolished in favour of an all-powerful unitary national government devolving local powers to local regions. In Labor lore, the federal system 'protected property' through weaker government.

Yet another level of Labor administration was the state-based union assemblies of the capital city trades halls and their regional affiliates. The names and constitutions varied from state to state. The senior body was the venerable Labor Council (later Unions NSW). Its Victorian equivalent was the Trades Hall Council (THC). Brisbane had the Trades and Labor Council. These assemblies, typically held one night a week, decided joint policies, often of a fairly technical nature, for the members, such as the detail of state industrial awards and the far-ranging conditions for state government employees. They also oversaw administration of the trades halls, where in the 50s most individual unions had their small, low cost offices, unadorned except perhaps by union banners. Usually the number of delegates per union was capped, perhaps at four, so that big unions were less dominant than in the ALP. More white collar unions also affiliated to the State councils than to the ALP. In some states and from time to time, the AWU did not affiliate at all. Unlike with the ALP, Communist Party members were free to be Labor Council delegates and many of the more visibly great union clashes of the era took place there. The communists were trained to a loud, violent style of oratory and contempt for their opponents. Often on perhaps a Thursday night during the Cold War, they and their opponents could shake the sturdy trades hall buildings to the rafters with rhetoric, even over relatively apolitical questions of industrial affairs. The grand old man of the trades halls was J.V 'Vic' Stout, secretary of the Victorian THC since 1939 and a veteran of Labor politics since before World War I. Stout earned much respect for his doughty work in fighting off communist attempts in the 1940s to capture control of the THC, but in the 50s he increasingly was perceived as 'difficult' and having stayed on too long. The Communist Party's greatest prize was the Brisbane Trades Hall, where its member, Alex Macdonald, was secretary. One factor there was that the AWU kept apart from the Trades Hall.

The Australian Council of Trades Unions was the national equivalent of the state labor councils. Delegates to its two-yearly Congress, each held in a different city, mainly came from the Federal or National unions rather than state and local branches. The then small ACTU head office was located in Melbourne opposite the Trades Hall in Lygon Street, Carlton. In a typical arrangement, the ALP state office was located in the Trades Hall. These accommodation arrangements reflected the short pockets and low financial horizons of the Labor Movement, but not surprisingly, many well-wishers wondered if a little more distance might make it all somewhat less incestuous and damp down some of the both hostilities and chumminess.

Chapter 3

1954

Nineteen fifty-four should have been the gentlest of years for Australia. With postwar shortages and the Korean conflict over, and memories of the depression and war fading, a mood of justified optimism was replacing tension and fear. Prosperity had returned, indicating that the long-held concern that depression would return after the war was not justified. The era of suburban sprawl, city-centre glass houses, Holden cars and baby-boomers packing out the schools had arrived. A visit from the young Queen Elizabeth II in February–March, the first to Australia by a reigning monarch, seemed to complete the benign mood. Then into this tranquil scene a mysterious Providence thrust one of the most bizarre sequences of events in Australian history.

On 13 April 1954, the day before parliament was due to rise for the elections, Prime Minister R.G. Menzies announced that Vladimir Mikhailovich Petrov, third secretary to the Soviet embassy in Canberra since 1951, had sought political asylum in Australia. Evatt happened to be at a function in Sydney and was furious at not being told in advance of the defection. However, Labor supported legislation for a royal commission to investigate the documents Petrov handed over to ASIO (Australian Security Intelligence Organisation). There were suggestions that Australians had provided sensitive information to the Soviets. Petrov's main motive had been fear for his life. He had been a secret police agent, allegedly in the faction loyal to Lavrenti Beria, the police chief deposed after Stalin's death. The Australian government paid Petrov an initial sum to help him establish a life in Australia. ASIO had told Petrov there would be more money later in exchange for 'good' documents.

Suspicions began to grow in Labor ranks that Menzies had arranged for Petrov to defect just before the election in the hope of embarrassing and dividing his opponents, as had happened with the Communist Party ban and the double-dissolution crisis of 1951. Some weeks earlier, a Sydney newspaper reported that Menzies would 'pull a white rabbit out of his hat' for the election, and Labor members speculated that this might be it. This is not the place to analyse the 'Petrov affair' but, while the timing was interesting, the evidence does not support the conspiracy theory many Laborites clung to for decades. Nevertheless, pre-election incidents continued, with Mrs Petrov deciding to seek Australian protection at Darwin airport on 20 April and the royal commission opening on 5 May. Dramatic pictures of a terrified Mrs Petrov and her Soviet guards at Sydney and Darwin airports crystallised the Cold War for many Australians and it seems to have been the first political event the young baby-boomers noticed. Despite this the Petrov defection did not play a major part in the election campaign, though the deputy prime minister (and Country Party leader) Arthur Fadden, claimed that the coalition would best 'carry out with the rigour of the law' the findings of the inquiry.

The election campaign was much more about Evatt's promise to abolish the means test on age pensions and to increase pensions by 25 per cent, which he announced in opening his campaign on 7 May. According to estimates, Evatt's promises overall would have increased commonwealth expenditure by a third to half in one year. He suggested no practical way of funding them. Evatt did not consult properly with his party about these promises and they were a surprise to his financial spokesmen, Tom Burke and Frank Crean. They also brought public criticism from Victorian Bill Bourke, who told an election meeting he was 'not happy about everyone getting pensions'. Menzies called the Evatt policy speech a 'jumble of nonsense' and Fadden spoke of a 'crackpot, jackpot financial revolution'. In an agitated radio broadcast, his voice trembling with anger, Evatt retaliated: 'These are the people who dare to criticise me, the smearers, the slanderers ...' Evatt had further added to his promises by secretly seeking out Santamaria and promising aid for Catholic schools and for land settlement.

The election on 29 May brought victory for the Menzies-Fadden coalition by a slim margin. Labor won 50.03 per cent of the vote but small differences in a number of seats and concentration of the Labor vote in industrial areas made the difference. For Evatt, now sixty, his dream to be prime minister was now unlikely. He had shown little leadership or flair for winning public support in his three years as leader: the means-test promise and his general campaigning style discredited him and divisions over communism and Catholicism were still building within the party.

Division was also developing among the Catholic bishops over the dominating role of the Movement. Laymen were intended to run the Catholic Action organisations and the Movement, and the bishops, in principle, had limited authority over them. The major issue, however, was Santamaria's intention to use the Movement as a disciplined force to influence Australian politics. One group of bishops led by Dr Mannix, the venerable Melbourne prelate, was prepared to leave the Movement free to pursue Santamaria's visionary strategy. Another, led by James Carroll, the new auxiliary bishop of Sydney, was not. Carroll came from a strong Labor family. He was horrified at the potential of the Movement for division in the Church, the party and the general community. He wanted to trim it back to a purely industrial body. This division became evident at bishops' meetings between the end of 1953 and September 1954. For Santamariaites the overwhelming question, despite the arguments about authority, was the claimed threat from the north to Australia's security. The deepening division was to be the most bitter and longest-lasting split Australian Catholics would ever experience.

Yet another complicated bit of unravelling was under way by mid-1954 in the ranks of the Industrial Groups supporters. On the one hand the Industrial Groups wanted the Federal Conference of January 1955 to give them a national organisation. This would allow them to be better organised in the unions for the expected fightback by the communists. The ironworkers at Whyalla, South Australia, were one example of a critical body of workers outside the formal reach of ALP Groups. But on the other hand the Groups were losing key supporters. The most critical was the large Australian Workers' Union, which covered rural workers and had influence over several other unions.

The fairly petty, if intricate, politics of this rumpus were soon to affect the nation: the AWU held the balance of power in New South Wales Labor between the grouper faction and its various opponents – and had the potential to hold it nationally. The general secretary of the AWU, Tom Dougherty, had once been fearful of communist intervention in his union and backed the Groups. Now he feared that the Movement and its friends were out to undermine him. This fear was focused on Jack Kane, assistant secretary and Groups organiser of the New South Wales ALP and Frank Rooney, Country Organiser. Both were active in the Movement and showed their loyalty to Santamaria rather than the Sydney bishops. Both were skilled industrial operators. The groupers were campaigning for 'clean' unionism, with freely available court-controlled ballots, after their success in the courts against communist ballot rigging. Dougherty's AWU was not famous for the purity of its ballots – the ballot papers for AWU elections were printed in the union newspaper and collected by paid organisers.

Dougherty came to believe that Kane and Rooney were now conspiring with other AWU officials to defeat him, though there has never been evidence to justify this suspicion. Several other non-communist union officials in Melbourne, too, came to fear the Movement, not so much for its ideology as for its organising capacity in union elections. The veteran Jack Lang, whose biting weekly paper *Century* influenced many Labor supporters, also swung about from an anti-communist stance to one of hostility towards the groupers. Soon after, Evatt, possibly nervous of a move against him by Calwell, was to change sides and join Dougherty and the other anti-groupers.

After the election of May 1954 Evatt began to believe that the Petrov defections were a conspiracy by Menzies and ASIO to rob him of victory at the polls. In August and September 1954, in an extraordinary performance in front of the royal commission, he made his allegations public.

Three members of Evatt's personal staff were named in Petrov documents as providing minor information to Soviet embassy personnel. Press secretary Fergan O'Sullivan was named as having given a Russian news representative gossip about the frailties of Canberra press gallery members. Allan Dalziel and Albert Grundeman, Evatt's private secretary and assistant secretary respectively, were also named in the Russian documents as sources of information. O'Sullivan admitted to writing the screed on the press gallery in 1951, before he joined Evatt, to help the Russians get their viewpoint across. Otherwise all three denied having given help and the three judges accepted this. In any case, the alleged information, including the document on the press gallery, amounted to little more than Canberra pub gossip, although Evatt, appearing as barrister for his staff, used the opportunity to develop his conspiracy charge.

Labor caucus members watched Evatt with some alarm. Already about 25 per cent of them had voted against him when the new post-election caucus assembled. Tom Burke, MP for Perth (father of 1980s Western Australian premier Brian Burke) stood against Evatt as a protest at lack of consultation over the means test promise. This was a high vote for somebody outside the leadership group and it added to Evatt's deepening sense of insecurity. Then, as their leader's allegations at the Petrov inquiry daily became more serious, the parliamentarians began to think about replacing him. Evatt's role as leader of the opposition continued while he was before the inquiry and he used the opportunity to pursue his Petrov obsession. On 7 September the judges withdrew Evatt's right to appear saying his dual roles had compromised his responsibilities.

Evatt strode angrily from the furore of the caucus room the next day when some members began to question him after he made a long speech about Petrov. The Ward group, looking to outmanoeuvre Calwell for the succession, took the high ground of supporting Evatt. Ward tried to force a vote of confidence but it led to a scuffle among angry members. The next week Evatt returned – without consultation – to the inquiry and unsuccessfully sought leave to appear again. With the Ward group tactically becoming his defenders, bitter left-right clashes followed in caucus. Beneath the turmoil many members were worrying about Evatt's sanity.

In the crude politics of immediate survival, shorn of principle, Evatt's obvious step was to abandon the listing grouper ship to his closest rival, Calwell, and jump aboard the refitted anti-grouper vessel. He did this at the New South Wales Labor Day dinner at Sydney Town Hall on 2 October 1954. The principle of common justice had become a crucial question, he told the cheering diners. Tom Dougherty praised the address as did other significant union leaders. That weekend Evatt began drafting a momentous press statement in which he extended the conspiracy against him to the groupers and Movement. He issued it on Tuesday 5 October. One commentator called it 'Dr Evatt's hydrogen bomb' and it sparked off the greatest explosion in the history of Australian Labor.

The nub of Evatt's charge was that a small group had infiltrated caucus and subverted his and Chifley's leaderships. 'It seems certain that the activities of this small group are largely directed from outside the Labor Movement,' he said. 'The Melbourne *News Weekly* appears to act as their organ. A serious situation exists.'

The statement had a certain plausibility and was what much of the more leftward or Protestant-minded sections of the community believed – that Catholic Action was exerting an unhealthy, subversive and well-organised, though clandestine, influence. As is usual in conspiracy beliefs, however, the facts were more mundane. The Victorian MPs Stan Keon (Yarra) and Jack Mullens (Gellibrand) were close to the Movement and reflected its views, though Keon could also be a scornful critic. These two and a couple of others were part of a lunching group with Santamaria at Melbourne's Cafe Latin. The Movement had had some influence in the grouper faction, but by October 1954 in New South Wales most had been lost following the bishops' split. This Evatt knew. On questions Santamaria looked on as vital, such as foreign policy and land settlement, the Movement had great difficulty in having much effect against the typical pragmatism and narrow interests of the ALP right. The idea that Santamaria could control or sway large numbers of Labor politicians and union officials, though widely alleged, was fanciful.

Evatt announced on 5 October that 'having in view the absolute necessity for real, and not sham solidarity', he would bring his allegations before the next meeting of the federal executive. It was not Evatt's statement alone that brought about the intervention, but it acted as a catalyst to bring together dissident unions at the Sydney and Melbourne trades halls. In Melbourne, up to twenty-seven affiliated unions (the number varied between twenty-two and twenty-seven) called on the federal executive to 'review' the Victorian branch of the ALP and a similar number called for intervention in New South Wales. Both were coalitions of the left wing, often communist-influenced, unions and a 'centre' group dominated by the AWU. The New South Wales grouping called itself the 'Steering Committee', the name which flowed on to the New South Wales left faction of the party for decades later. The majority of the so-called 'pro-Evatt' grouping in Victoria became, fifteen years later, the underpinning of the 'Socialist Left'.

By 1954, Communist Party union strength had waned. It could not control more than 15-20 per cent of votes in combined gatherings. The vote it could hope to influence at ALP conferences was even less since some communist unions did not affiliate with the ALP or affiliated on an artificially low membership. Unions with officials sympathetic or obligated to communist officials might have added another 10-15 per cent of the vote in Labor councils. The left unions therefore had the potential, with enough incentive, to increase their strength in the ALP. The balance of power, however, would still lie with the 'centre' unions around the AWU and, in Victoria, the ageing secretary of the Trades Hall Council, Vic Stout. The 'centre' had varied motives, but the dominating one was the battle for survival in trade union politics. Alliances and animosities of industrial or interstate origin and personalities came into it as much as the touchy religious sectarian background.

The federal executive, which then comprised two delegates from each state, became the engine driving the split. The executive's job was to administer the Party, usually in the administrative rather than parliamentary sense, between meetings of the Federal Conference, the supreme ruling body. At its more controversial, though successful over time, the Executive had intervened several times in New South Wales during the disputes associated with J.T. Lang between the wars. Historically its role had been conciliatory. Over the decades it enjoyed a close association with the federal leader, especially with Chifley. Sensible leaders no doubt thought it wise not to give the executive too much of a taste of power. Only in Evatt's day did the executive's role become contentious.

The annual or triennial Labor conference in each state, dominated by union delegations, selected the delegates to both the Executive and the Federal conferences. The usual custom was for the state secretary and leader, or their representatives, to be the two federal executive delegates. A balance of union officials, parliamentarians and party administrators was sought in the six-member Federal Conference delegations.

A special meeting of the federal executive in Canberra on 27 October 1954 heard the various charges relating to the Victorian branch and decided on a formal inquiry. This began in the then Australian Council of Trade Unions boardroom in Lygon Street, Carlton, opposite the Melbourne Trades Hall, on 10 November. It lasted a hundred tangled hours but proved little more than what everybody already knew – there was a fight on. The original allegations against Keon, Mullens and Bourke became lost in a miscellany of allegations against the Victorian central executive, some of which suggested that the 'Movement' might have influence and that the executive and 'grouper' forces could at times be overbearing. Nevertheless, the federal executive decided by seven votes to five on 3 December to dismiss the Victorian central executive. It ordered a federally supervised special conference of the Victorian branch for the weekend of 26–27 February 1955 to elect a new state executive. It added that delegates would be accepted who did not have the usual Victorian qualification of two years' continuous membership of the ALP. It also ordered an end to support for the Industrial Groups. It postponed the Federal Conference due for Hobart in January until March, after the Victorian special conference.

Why did the executive make this draconian decision, in the absence of more substantial evidence of the alleged 'outside' influence or control? The acting federal president on the day, F.E. 'Joe' Chamberlain, state secretary in Western Australia, told the Victorians that a 'frame of mind' adverse to them had been created. This, in a nutshell, was it. The political pressures were so great that the majority of delegates felt something had to be done. Most were convinced that the Movement, through the Industrial Groups, local ALP branches, sympathisers in the clergy and hierarchy and through *News Weekly*, exerted an unacceptable influence. But this was only half the story. When the delegates began to weaken in the absence of convincing evidence, Dougherty threatened that the AWU would withdraw its affiliation to the ALP, while the other dissident unions also threatened to break and form an 'Industrial Labor Party'. Another over-riding consideration was the desire to change the Victorian delegation to the 1955 Federal Conference. This was the conference that would decide whether to disband the Industrial Groups or give them a federal structure – and, in effect, national control. The Calwell – Ward jostling to succeed Evatt was a strong background influence.[†]

† The lack of evidence and hesitation about proceeding was reported in the press at the time, *The Age* of 6 December 1954, p. 2, has a summary of the intervention.

Divisions grew more strident and extreme through the summer. One of the most telling weapons against the Right was a 'leaked' speech, 'the Movement of Ideas', which Santamaria gave to a Movement conference early in 1954. He made it clear that he expected his supporters ('us') to influence 'them' (the ALP) in the battle of ideas to secure a pro-American, pro-defence foreign policy. He said they should try to replace the 'soft', 'Chifley Legend' foreign policy with a pro-American 'Curtin Legend'. While this was fair political game, the AWU and left unions also resorted to lurid pamphleteering attacking 'Santa-stiletto' which was designed to raise anti-Catholic, anti-Mediterranean feelings – Santamaria's parents were Italian. In January Dougherty and his lieutenants attacked the enemy at the annual AWU conference, blurring the distinction between the ALP Groups and the Movement. Most of this seems to have been a deliberate strategy of piling on the pressure ever since Evatt's statement, inflaming ALP opinion (and the general public's) against the Industrial Groups and the Movement and confusing the two as much as possible to keep the pressure on Evatt and other waverers. Neither side trusted Evatt and he had shown signs of retreat at the Melbourne inquiry when he did not prove or press his charges. Yet the only way Evatt could keep his leadership and stave off a Calwell challenge was to be out in the front of the anti-grouper campaign.

On the other side, the Industrial Groups supporters became determined to fight back against what they considered a monstrous injustice. The Communist Party, too, showed an interest in the outcome, contributing to the heat and division, which alarmed many groupers. Two stories spread which further caused concern: that parliamentarians such as Keon, of the Victorian central executive, and Frank Scully, a state counterpart, would be expelled when the new Victorian executive took over; and that non-members of the ALP, possibly even Communist Party members, would be admitted to the special conference as delegates. In general, groupers formed the impression that the federal executive majority would stop at nothing to win.

In this inflamed climate the Movement's influence increased, its network of reliable members a ballast for the Right. Its influence in the Church was a powerful weapon, with Archbishop Mannix (then ninety) speaking publicly in support of the Industrial Groups. In a compromise outcome, though, the Movement's influence would be drastically weakened because it had too many enemies. With its tendency to take the more extreme view about communist strength the Movement believed the Communist Party would gain immeasurable strength from the split emerging in the ALP and would use it to assist the downward thrust from China, directed from

DR EVATT DENOUNCES VICTORIAN MP'S GROUP—'TRAITORS TO PARTY'

WEATHER BUREAU: Westerly wind change preceded by some showers and thunderstorms. Cooler temperatures following.

The Argus

FOUNDED 1846

WEDNESDAY OCTOBER 6 1954

Telephone: FO411 Price 4d. (By Airmail, 5d.)
Registered at the G.P.O., Melbourne, for transmission by post as a newspaper.

Sydney, Tuesday

IN a sensational statement tonight, Dr. Evatt Federal Opposition Leader, denounced the "subversive" element in a minority group of Labor Party members, located particularly in Victoria.

Dr. Evatt announced that, in the interests of Labor unity, he would report the group to the next meeting of the Federal Executive on November 8.

He would do this with a view to "appropriate action" being taken by the Party's ruling body, the Federal Labor conference, next January.

Dr. Evatt said the Melbourne paper, "News-Weekly," appeared to act as the group's organ.

He did not name any members of the Party in his statement.

Dr. Evatt said that Labor had made gains at the recent Federal election in every State except Victoria.

"One factor told heavily against us — the attitude of a small minority group of Labor members, particularly in Victoria," he said.

'Disloyal group'

"This group, since 1949, has become increasingly disloyal to the Labor movement and to Labor leadership."

Dr. Evatt said the group had adopted methods which resembled both Communist and Fascist infiltration of larger groups.

"Some of these groups have created an almost intolerable situation, calculated to deflect the Labor movement from the pursuit of established Labor objectives and ideals. "Whenever it suits their real aims, one or more of them never hesitates to attack or subvert Labor policy or Labor leadership.

"A striking example of this at the Federal election was the attack on Labor's proposal to abolish the means test.

"That proposal had been approved, not only by myself, but by authorised representatives of the Federal executive, the A.C.T.U., A.W.U., and leaders of the Parliamentary Labor Party in both Houses.

"In spite of that, there were further attacks on the agreed policy. These attacks were eagerly seized on by anti-Labor parties, as though by a preconceived plan, and advertised from one end of the country to the other."

Dr. Evatt said that Labor gains at the last Federal election were achieved by the self-sacrifice of tens of thousands of voluntary workers for Labor.

They were achieved, despite the thinly veiled use against Labor of the opening speech before the Petrov Commission, which seemed to be distant many poles apart from the truth of the matter so far as it has been more recently revealed by the sworn evidence of many witnesses.

'Subversive'

Dr. Evatt added:

"Since the elections nothing has been done officially to deal with those responsible for the disloyal and subversive actions to which I refer.

In addition, it is my clear belief that in crucial constituencies, members of the

● Continued on Page 5.

The Split began when Federal Opposition Leader Dr Evatt issued a controversial statement to the press on 5 October 1954, reported on front pages around Australia next morning.

The Argus, 6 October 1954

The right and left wings of the ALP were soon at war after the Party's Leader, Dr H.V. Evatt called it on with his incendiary press statement on 5 October 1954.

Daily Telegraph, 8 October 1954

POSTPONED

It was a critical moment when Deputy Labor Leader Arthur Calwell decided not to oppose his embattled leader, Dr Evatt, for the Leadership over Evatt's attack on the ALP Industrial Group faction and Evatt's controversial appearances before the Petrov espionage Royal Commission.

Finey, *Daily Telegraph*, 14 October 1954

"They're a'goin' that-a way!"

Neither the right nor left of the ALP seemed to want their Federal Leader, Dr Evatt, as the Split he sparked off deepened. Hopalong Cassidy was a Wild West film character star of the day.

Tanner, *Daily Telegraph*, 12 November 1954

Moscow. The Movement's slogan was that it was 'Five Minutes to Midnight' for Australia's survival as a free democracy. It produced an exceedingly pessimistic analysis of the likely 'numbers' for the forthcoming Victorian conference.

The idea began to develop that grouper forces should boycott the special conference to avoid giving it 'respectability'. Instead, the groupers would challenge the special conference rules in the courts and send a rival delegation to the March Federal Conference. If all else failed, they would adopt the tactic their opponents had used earlier and threaten to and even form a breakaway Labor Party. The first of these options, the legal challenge, was not successful and neither was the second because the federal executive outmanoeuvred them. The third option was the course followed. It was to colour Australian politics for the next twenty years.

Some of those involved later regretted the decision the outgoing Victorian central executive took in the bitter heat of January 1955 to boycott the special conference. Some saw an element of self interest in the Movement's bleak analysis. They conceded, however, that as long as such determined opponents controlled the federal executive, political life for the groupers was precarious.

The decision to boycott also split grouper ranks. Two major defectors were the Victorian secretary of the ALP, Denis 'Dinny' Lovegrove, the talented, bitter ex-communist who had been the anti-communist brains of the Melbourne Trades Hall since the 1930s, and Ted Peters, MP for Scullin and until then an ardent Industrial Groups supporter. Peters was close to Calwell and his defection was a signal that Calwell – the most senior Victorian Catholic parliamentarian – would not be joining any breakaway party. Without Calwell and Lovegrove, the most senior non-Catholic grouper, the attempted defiance of the federal power would merely seem the extremist Catholicism it was suspected of being. Calwell and Lovegrove foresaw the Protestant majority of voters mistrusting and rejecting such a party; they just did not think it could win.

The boycotting executive also lost its 'moderate' minority, which included the premier John Cain and his deputy Bill Galvin; the secretary of the ACTU, Reg Broadby; and a former ACTU president, Percy Clarey. Most of these had once supported the Groups but now felt their time was up. They expected more left representation on the new Victorian executive, which would give the moderates the balance of power, while tilting the Federal Conference against the groupers. This was senator Kennelly's bold strategy for reuniting the party, which they accepted. Cain emphasised the importance of working within the rules and told colleagues, 'It'll all be over in six weeks.' He was wrong.

The strengths and weaknesses of the groupers' decision to boycott can be seen by an analysis of the special conference. Two hundred and forty-nine delegates attended, compared to about 400 at the June 1954 conference. Only fifteen delegates were not members of the ALP, the big factor the groupers feared. (Its purpose was to allow the left unions to affiliate with bigger membership numbers and send only absolutely 'reliable' delegates.) Some groupers later believed that by rigorous organisation they could have marshalled a majority. Perhaps the more likely outcome of attending was that the new centre-left alliance would have won control of the executive and withdrawn ALP support for the Groups. It might have expelled or worked to end the Labor endorsement of a couple of right-wing parliamentarians. However, most of the groupers and their organisation would have survived, if battered and bloodied. The centre faction would probably have sought moderation on most points. The difference in the potential line-up between 1955 and the early 1950s was that the Left and centre, with federal support and the smell of victory, had strengthened their organisation and won the support of others who would once have backed the Groups. But the grouper numbers in the big unions they had won back and a strong Movement representation from the branches would still have been there.

The ALP Left was now more under communist influence than earlier. After its big defeats in the Federated Ironworkers' Association, Federated Clerks' Union and other unions, the Communist Party had adopted a strategy of building up a bigger left wing within the ALP, with which it could find greater public acceptance. The Communist Party's initiative in rebuilding the Left was to be so successful that the Socialist Left absorbed the splintered communists. But this was to take many years.

Two bitterly antagonistic bodies now appeared in Victoria, both claiming to be the true central executive of the ALP: the 'new' elected by the special conference and the 'old', the majority of the executive elected by the 1954 state conference.

The 'new executive elected by the special conference reflected the distinctive anti-politician background of the Melbourne Trades Hall. Unlike in most states, especially NSW and Queensland, Labor had rarely been in office in Victoria, where the State electoral distribution was skewed to conservative rural districts. What periods of office Labor had held had mostly been through support from the Country Party on the cross-benches in return for concessions. At other times it had supported minority Country Party governments. Such dealing was probably the best it could do in the circumstances, but it did not win the hearts and minds of trade union officials, many of whom – moderate as well as militant – at best gave little priority to Labor governing and often disdained the political wing. They did not have the natural acceptance of Labor government common in Sydney and Brisbane. Ironically, the Labor Government elected in 1952 but destroyed in 1955 was the first in the Victoria's history to enjoy a parliamentary majority and also one of its best performing. Local Labor branch membership and finances were also strong. The groupers were proud of this success under their administration. But success in politics also brings onerous responsibilities.

A new division between pro- and anti-groupers had opened on the floor of the Trades Hall Council as well as the ALP conference, replacing that previously over the communists, the invective little less bitter. As well as issues involving the State Government, fear of the grouper organisation's potential in union elections, and perhaps religious sensibilities, were potent; the unions were less Catholic than the ALP and Freemasonry was whispered as a contributor to the discord. A separate brawl in Sydney between the groupers and the AWU and Transport Workers' Union, described in Chapter 5, flowed into and aggravated the Victorian troubles. Opponents found the groupers arrogant and intransigent. The young, ambitious Federal MP Stan Keon emerged as a Group leader in both forums and was suspected, probably not without reason, as leading secretive intervention in selected non-communist unions vulnerable to takeover. The groupers, fearing that part of the moderates were now becoming uncomfortably close to the Trades Hall communists and Left, wanted to build up their own base of support. Though affable and witty off-stage, Keon was a master of shrill, scornful oratory which deepened the divisions. He was perceived as a 'Catholic Action hatchet man'.

This was the fevered atmosphere in which Federal Executive intervention unrolled. However, unlike in NSW later when the press reported daily on Split activity, the Victorian wheeling and dealing in the summer of 1954–55 was secretive and the sharp swing to the Left at the Special Conference was a shock, a 'coup' in one version. It is difficult to avoid the conclusion that Vic Stout, the veteran THC secretary, did a deal with the Communist Party, his bitter enemy only a few years before, to support the left-wing unions in return for holding his job; he was nearly 70, past his best; did not want to retire; and his usual allies were divided or uncertain. He and the moderate unions backing him would have the balance of power in the State ALP and the THC – a position much desired by politicians – in return for a hard line against the groupers. Also involved was the prospect of Victoria being the nucleus for a left-wing Labor Party led by Eddie Ward; the Adelaide MP Clyde Cameron, who was becoming Ward's organiser and 'numbers man' was active behind the scenes in Victoria throughout the crisis. A 'moderate' faction headed by senator Kennelly and 'Mick' Jordan, the Assistant THC secretary and Stout's eventual successor, was solidly defeated at the Special Conference. Kennelly's grand strategy to use Evatt's statement to tame the groupers and then unite the Party under Calwell had backfired!

On 13 March 1955 the two bitterly antagonistic Victorian executives dispatched rival delegations to the Federal Conference due to open at the Hobart Trades Hall the next day. The 'old', grouper delegates hoped that the other five states would provide a majority to accept them, while the 'new' anti-grouper delegation expected the federal executive to use its credentialling power. The 'old' delegates relied strongly on a 1927 precedent, when the conference chose between rival delegations from New South Wales. This time the federal executive had met ahead of the conference, however and accepted the credentials of the 'new' Victorians only.

This decision swung the conference to the Left, although seventeen delegates when presented with the executive decision on credentials boycotted the conference and considered, though did not proceed with, holding a rival conference. As in Victoria six weeks earlier, the decision to boycott was taken in heat and some later regretted it. As it was, the conference had to move to a church hall, where police could be called in against trespassers, because of the hostility of the Hobart Trades Hall secretary. All six South Australians, the 'new' Victorians, one Queenslander and split delegations from Tasmania and Western Australia took part in the 'church hall conference'. The remainder – six from New South Wales, five Queenslanders, four Western Australians and two Tasmanians – boycotted.

The Victorian branch now approached the brink. With intense feelings mounting the new executive set about asserting its authority over the parliamentarians, while each executive declared the other 'bogus'. Four state ministers, thirteen state parliamentarians, seven federal MP and one senator (who later changed) showed their allegiance to the 'old' executive by attending a 'support' meeting it had called for on 25 March. The state parliamentary Labor Party split 32–17 on 29 March over a motion to support the 'new'. That night the 'new' executive suspended the twenty-four parliamentarians who had given their support to the 'old' executive from ALP membership. It gave them until 7 April, the date of the next 'new' executive meeting, to switch allegiance. They did not switch and on the 'Night of the Knife', 7 April 1955, the executive expelled from the ALP eighteen state parliamentarians, twenty-three endorsed Labor candidates for state seats at the election due later in 1955, seven federal parliamentarians, seven Melbourne city councillors and eleven members of the 'old' executive. In total, 104 members were expelled from the ALP. Soon local branches across the state were riven in outrage against one side or the other. It had taken a lot of pressure, including religious and tribal, to get so many reluctant politicians across a career destroying line, but many had genuinely believed the 'old' executive would win,

By this stage, a split had become evident in the 'new' executive between trade union officials, whether left or 'centre', who voted as a bloc, and 'moderates' comprising parliamentarians such as Cain and Kennelly. This division reflected the prevailing factional pattern in the Trades Hall Council. The left-wing unions were dominating in a way they could hardly have dreamt of six months earlier.

The schism quickly spread into the state government. The Liberal leader of the opposition, Henry Bolte, moved a shrewdly worded motion of no confidence in the Cain government when parliament resumed on 19 April. The expelled group crossed the floor at 4.20 a.m. on 20 April to vote with the opposition and the first majority Labor government in Victoria's history fell by thirty-four votes to twenty-three. Although the Cain government had had its tensions, the split that destroyed it was – in questions of state government – about nothing. Amid unprecedented bitterness by Labor people, Bolte became premier by a comfortable margin at the 28 May election, six months before it was due. The expelled dissidents had adopted the name Australian Labor Party (Anti-Communist) and won 12.6 per cent of the vote, losing all but one seat. (In 1957 this group became the Democratic Labor Party.) Cain Labor won 32.6 per cent, the Liberals (including their own dissidents) 41.7 per cent and the Country Party 9.5 per cent. The vindictiveness and hysteria on both sides of the two Labor camps led to them breaking with usual practice and giving most of their second preferences to the Liberals. Bolte was to remain premier for seventeen years and Labor was not to regain the Treasury benches in Victoria for twenty-seven years.

Feelings were similar in New South Wales, where Evatt returned after the Hobart debacle to mount desperate public attacks on his own right, depicting them as controlled by Santamaria and fascists. However, premier Joe Cahill took the lead behind the scenes to prevent a split. Memories of the bitterness and fruitlessness of the Labor faction-fighting between the wars were still keen. The developing rejection of the Movement in the Catholic Church was another major reason for caution. A third was the continuing support of the 'moderate' unions at Trades Hall for the pro-

Group executive. Whatever their personal or religious feelings about the Movement, the leaders of these smaller unions preferred the devil they knew; they did not want to leap into the unknown with Moscow and the AWU. The complex Trades Hall faction fight that so aggravated the situation in Melbourne just did not exist. Prodded by federal officials and the AWU, the New South Wales state executive agreed to a special conference there in August 1955. But this time the pro-groupers attended, and, by a slither of a margin, won.

In September 1955 the Petrov commission report was tabled in the federal parliament. The commissioners said they accepted the evidence of the Petrov as truth, thus implicitly rejecting Evatt's allegations of forgery and fabrication. They also found that there had been Soviet espionage in Australia in the immediate postwar years, with leakages of information from a section of the Department of External Affairs. This was when Evatt was minister, though the incidents reflected more on his judgment than allegiance. Opening the debate on the report in the house on 19 October, Evatt made the extraordinary statement that he had written to Molotov, the Soviet foreign minister, about the validity of the Petrov documents and the reply (by an official, not Molotov personally) had said that documents were falsifications. This was Evatt placing a routine denial of espionage by a semi-hostile totalitarian foreign government above the findings of three Australian judges, who had heard many laborious hours of evidence and cross-examination.

On 26 October, after a blistering reply to Evatt's statement, Menzies announced an election for 10 December. Although he did not have to go to the polls until 1957, Menzies said there was a need to get the Senate and house elections back into alignment after the double dissolution of 1951. Yet it was likely that Labor's and Evatt's disarray was also a reason.

For most of 1955 the seven expelled Victorians, who included Keon, Mullens and Bourke, and the main Labor Party had attacked each other with smears and allegations, in what at times was great parliamentary theatre. These seven, who ran under the ALP (Anti-Communist) banner, at the election got 17.8 per cent of the vote in Victoria, as against 37 per cent for 'Evatt Labor'. All lost their seats. However, the assistant secretary of the 'old' Victorian ALP, Frank McManus, won a six-year term in the Senate. He already had a colleague in Tasmanian senator George Cole, whom the AWU had suspended from the ALP for boycotting the Hobart conference. Cole had then crossed to the anti-communists.

The Liberals were the clear winners in 1955. The national Labor vote fell, though not by the margin that might have been expected, and Labor lost four seats altogether. More deeply, the split in the ALP soon spread beyond Victoria – over related but still substantially different issues – to New South Wales in 1956 and Queensland in 1957. As a consequence of the Split, over the next nine years Menzies was only ever in electoral trouble once.

Chapter 4

Bob Santamaria

Bartholomew Augustine Michael ('Bob' as he was usually known) Santamaria attracted more harsh epithets than almost anybody in Australian public life, while some admirers thought he was a saint. But over the years a growing middle ground of public opinion conceded that he had made a substantial and unique contribution to the nation's affairs. Santamaria's role was twofold; as Director of Catholic Action in Australia and President of its offshoot, the Movement, which became the National Civic Council in 1957; and as a commentator on national and world affairs.

His uniqueness lay in both the independent, often idiosyncratic perspective he brought to both roles and the extremely long period of his public contribution – it dated from 1936 until his death at 82 in 1998. He brought an extraordinary commitment and dedication to basic principles over this long period. He lived long enough to see many a former vehement critic on the Left come to admire him – but also to lose many former supporters in his Catholic community. The controversy surrounding him was partly because of his views, but much more because his of his life-long strategy of using the Catholic-based organisations he controlled – often quite tightly – to influence other organisations from the outside and the accompanying use of religion as a political power base.

He was of politics but not in them, tough and shrewd beneath a slightly pious exterior, persuasively charming and fluent, at ease with both the written and spoken word. His ego and desire to influence and win were as strong as anybody successful in public life. He never joined a political party but sought to influence them all. Short, chubby and cherubic, has was equally at home as a Catholic activist, Australian football barracker for his beloved Carlton, or making spaghetti for his big family of eight children (and later many grandchildren).

Santamaria was born in the inner Melbourne suburb of Brunswick on 14 August 1915 and grew up behind his Sicilian-born parents' licenced grocery in Sydney Road. About 20 minutes north of Melbourne University, in the twenty-first century it has the usual diverse 'gentrified' inner city mix, but in his youth was 90 per cent 'old Australian' or British working class, about 30 per cent of whom were Catholics of mainly Irish forebears. The experience of being an immigrant shopkeeper's son in this friendly but robust world of contending prejudices, pieties and folklore, cantankerous Labor politics, hard work or unemployment and poverty profoundly affected him. But Melbourne University down the road, where he studied arts/law to win major scholastic prizes, was another powerful influence.

His clerical sounding surname was to add awe to the 'Catholic Plot' excitement of the mid-1950s, but it may actually have been even more exotic. Many of the people of the Aeolian Islands, off Sicily, where his family originated had come centuries earlier from Spain, as Jews under pressure from the Inquisition. They often adopted conspicuously Catholic names to further distance themselves from persecution. This was not his handed-down family tradition, though.

Santamaria's most powerful ally in adult life was Melbourne Catholic Archbishop Daniel Mannix, who remained in office until he died at 99 in 1963. Mannix's support was a mixed blessing. Born in 1864, he was one of the last of the Irish bishops in Australia. The support of Mannix was another reason for later mistrust of Santamaria. Tall, austere, articulate, with a memorably biting wit that sometimes misfired, Mannix had earned over the years the ire of many Protestants and not a few Catholics. He became and remained a notable public figure from his arrival, aged 49, in 1913, at first with abrasive statements about State Aid to Catholic schools and Freemasonry and then about conscription for World War I and the war itself. In the 1920s he publicly supported the more radical wing of Irish nationalism, though he had in Ireland been perceived as a moderate. Protestants who remembered the earlier Mannix often thought of him as bitterly Irish and divisive, sneering hurtfully at the war to a community still raw after 60,000 war deaths and twice as many serious injuries. Was he an Irish-Australian hero? A divisive trouble-maker? Shy and reclusive in private, despite the headlines, did he really understand Australian society? Was he as wise as he looked? Was it just another tin ear? The debate still raged more than half a century after he died.

Like most bishops, Mannix became a strong anti-communist in the 1930s. There was much 'insider' speculation as to whether Santamaria or Mannix had the greater influence in the close partnership that developed; critics believed Santamaria at first cultivated the ageing Archbishop and later had excessive influence over him. Santamaria himself acknowledged that he was the son Mannix never had. He was eventually to be one of Mannix's many biographers.

The depression of the early 1930s, coming little more than a decade after the slaughter of World War I, brought a crisis of confidence in western democracy in Santamaria's most impressionable years. In the intellectually turbulent years of slow economic recovery, many students and academics were attracted to the Left, often communism. Others, including many Catholics, thought fascism a reasonable response – in Europe, though less so Australia – to the economic problems and lure of atheistic communism.

Another strong influence on the young Santamaria was the Campion Society. This was formed in Melbourne in 1931 to study Catholic culture and ideas and give laymen a role in church affairs. The germ of the political ideas that led a quarter of a century later to the Democratic Labor Party emerged in the Campion Society. A key influence in it was the writer, broadcaster and teacher Denys Jackson, an English immigrant convert to Catholicism, who exerted an extraordinary intellectual influence over Catholicism, particularly its public face, in Victoria for decades, though critics dismissed him as romantic, doctrinaire and eccentric. The Campions looked for distinctively Catholic solutions to the distress of the '30s in Papal Social Encyclicals and other Catholic social teaching, such as institutionalised cooperation between workers and employers and more land or private property for the workers. The young Campions saw such policies as the practical alternative to communism, the appeal of which grew rapidly after the depression.

The Campions saw themselves as involved in a struggle against international evil, manifested in atheism, 'materialist' secular society and world communism. They became one of the sources of an intense anti-communist mood which developed among Catholics as the appeal of communism quickened. The Campions tended to follow international trends in anti-communism, leading them to sympathy for rightist or fascist causes with a stridency many would later regret.

Such right-wing causes fitted the range of views acceptable in the non-Labor parties, but were anathema to most Labor people, in the 30s as at any time later. Nevertheless, most of the Campions saw themselves as Labor people; about two-thirds of Catholics then voted Labor. The Catholic Church of their time would be seen later, however, as 'right wing', dominated in most of the world by rigid traditionalists and often the upper classes. Especially in Europe it was in competition with the more secular and often anti-clerical Social Democratic parties, akin to Labor in Australia. In this view the Church – there was only one – was God's instrument on earth and God would shield it from error. Many Catholic writers argued that the Reformation and accompanying rise of Protestantism and capitalism had distorted European society; they looked back to the Middle Ages, with its dominating single church, feudal class structure and craft guilds as the ideal. It was a view that could become painful in Australia and similar countries. Typically, the Church was unenthusiastic about parliamentary democracy. In retrospect it could be seen as easing towards the centre after the trauma of the depression, but it was at first glacially slow movement that would take a generation.

In 1936 the Campions appointed Santamaria, then aged 20, as first editor of their monthly magazine, *Catholic Worker*, adopting an American name and inspiration. It was established to develop and publicise international Catholic social and foreign policy ideas and analyse how best to treat them in Australia. Critics sneered that, despite the name, it was written and read by middle class academics and professionals, but it won a quite large circulation.

In later years, Santamaria's organisations were often accused of in some ways resembling the Communist Party, their opponent, and this was true of the early *Catholic Worker*. It showed the same excited, conspiratorial, dogmatic style of journalism as the communist press and naïveté about societies abroad – especially, in the *Worker's* case, the Franco forces in the Spanish Civil War, Portugal and Austria in its alleged 'clerical fascist' phase. Santamaria's tendency was already evident to think markedly in theories and follow them through to extremes; and of an ever-present powerful enemy. It was a mind-set resembling that of many communist leaders. And like many highly intelligent people of theoretical and analytical bent, Santamaria sometimes could overlook the obvious.

Under him and his colleagues, the *Catholic Worker* fulminated against, as well as communism and socialism, capitalist industrial society – seen as exploitative – and materialism. Whether this could be classified as 'right' or 'left' was a good question. Santamaria much later said he had always perceived himself as an activist, presenting, developing and organising for ideas for society rather than as an originator or ideologist. His equally young colleagues thought of him as a leader, especially on foreign affairs; they mistrusted the seemingly Protestant, secular Australian press and were receptive to alternative views. They believed the secular press did not report adequately the unattractive face of Soviet Union communism.

Regarded earlier in the 1930s, as sympathetic to Mussolini's Italy, Santamaria was a prominent supporter of a more conciliatory approach to Nazi Germany, a viewpoint that saw the Soviet Union as the greater enemy of Western civilisation. This was the 'appeasement' view, common in Europe and the US as well as the Australian right – that the two totalitarian societies should be played off against each other. Santamaria's companions on a Melbourne 'peace' platform in mid-1939 included the coalition Prime Minister, R.G. Menzies and the Victorian Country Party Premier Albert Dunstan. (It was part of a pre-war Papal appeal for peace, the reason Mannix chose Santamaria, then 27, as organiser.) This meeting made useful political ammunition against him 15 years later. But Labor had also favoured appeasement, as ardently as Santamaria and the Right, though more from a pacifist, isolationist sentiment. While it cannot be seriously argued that Santamaria was ever a fascist, this sort of overriding urgency about communism and a tendency to see the world as facing catastrophe was to characterise much of his career.

In 1938 Archbishop Mannix supported him to be Assistant Director of the newly established Australian National Secretariat of Catholic Action, which developed out of the Campion Society. The bishops established this body to develop, organise, and coordinate a number of youth and lay organisations and further increase the role of the laity. Santamaria was appointed Lay Director of Catholic Action in 1947. The Church funded Catholic Action and placed it under a committee of bishops, with particular bishops overseeing the individual groupings. Some bishops were more enthusiastic than others and Sydney Archdiocese preferred to have its own similar local body. Catholic Action generally was an international movement intended mainly for training, or 'formation' of young Catholics to be more effective in society as individuals and more aware of Catholic culture.

Despite spiritual, educational goals, the Catholic Action national office in Melbourne soon became a centre for anti-communist organisation in the trade unions, at first informally in response to the rapid communist advances in the unions after the depression. Some senior ALP and union leaders had requested help to fend off the communist attacks. Mannix formally recognised and funded it as the Catholic Social Studies Movement in the early 1940s. It became known informally as 'the Movement' or 'the show'. The name was deliberately vague; it seemed hard to attack. The Australian bishops authorised the Movement nationally in 1945, when the Communist Party was almost able to control the ACTU Congress. Some of the social ideas from the '30s were grafted onto it as policies, partially adapted to Australian conditions. The individual dioceses paid for it. It status in relation to both official Catholic Action and the Church as a whole was undecided and remained unclear.

The beginnings were apparent early of bitter division, among Catholics as well as with Protestants. Catholic opponents believed Santamaria was too dominant and trying to make a political power base of the Church. Until the 1960s mistrust between Protestants and Catholics of each other's good will ran deep. A sense of both fear and rivalry, if not jealousy, was common. It was not a great problem if tact and fairness applied – but it often didn't. Many Protestants and the Left were deeply suspicious of Catholic Action from the start, seeing it as a backdoor attempt to impose clerical rule by training and organising Catholics to permeate public life. This was in fact an ideal Santamaria always clung to (though with himself as lay leader rather than the clergy). Santamaria himself later acknowledged that the 'Catholic Action' name might have been unintentionally provocative and unhelpful in the Australian context.

The Movement kept its work secret, as advised by several senior Labor and union leaders, who valued its role in reducing communist influence but feared disabling communist propaganda if its existence became public. Given wartime newsprint rationing and more pressing news from abroad, it is doubtful if a public announcement of the original work would have had much impact. However, there is secrecy and secrecy. Movement members took a pledge never to divulge its existence.

The Movement worked with anti-communist officials in the various trades halls and with the official ALP Industrial Groups which the ALP established in most states in the mid-40s to win communist-led unions back to affiliation with the ALP. At first it organised defensively for anti-communist members to attend their union meetings, which were otherwise poorly attended and used to increase communist control. It sought as far as possible to blur the distinction between itself and the official Industrial Groups. Its closest non-Catholic union contact was Victor Stout, Secretary of the Victorian Trades Hall Council, who was under constant attack from the Communist Party in the 1940s but was to eventually become such a crucial enemy. Stout and Movement organisers would talk about 'your (or our) friends'.

The deep secrecy added awe and was to be disastrous in the crisis of 1954. With their religiously based pledge not to disclose anything at all, Movement people appeared publicly deceitful when they suddenly had to grapple with how far to tell the truth, to explain the actual purpose of the Movement and its unclear relationship with the Church and Catholic Action. It was a big factor in turning possible moderate votes on the Federal Executive – and public opinion generally – against them. Standard public relations practice in the event of a possible scandal is to disclose the full truth as quickly as practical in order to avoid damagingly slow release under pressure and the impression of concealment. Less drastic secrecy and an emergency plan for disclosure might have produced a better result for the Movement in 1954–55. There would probably have not been a lot of public or political antagonism to a part-church, part-lay organisation intended only to assist the Industrial Groups. Few Australians had much sympathy for the 'red' unions, which seemed so bent on frequent disruptive strikes, though good communist leaders were often popular with their own member, regardless of politics.

Public relations was actually a big part of the Movement's problem in the mid-50s crisis. Stilted attempts to explain its main purpose sounded unconvincing, given the cloak and dagger drama of the allegations by its enemies. Its formal relationship with the Church and the ALP Groups, the ability to discipline its members, even the definition of a 'member' were all vague, as was the difference between its main purpose and the more exotic side-lights. Yet this very amorphousness had been what worked in the union fights – people working together for a common goal but coming from different directions.

In union elections, Movement members and supporters canvassed Catholic unionists in each parish to vote for anti-communist officials. The Movement encouraged them to stand for union office, including the unpaid and committee posts; and it provided secretarial, transport and rather modest financial help. Members usually said discreetly, if it arose, that they were working 'with the Industrial Groups'.

The Movement had a membership typically of about 5000 nationally, though more at the peak of the union battles. It consisted of secretively operating groups of typically about eight, but sometimes more, both in parishes and industries. It had the usual organisation of conferences, national and local executives and officers, but its employees dominated them. Santamaria was National President. His powerful personality, education and episcopal backing made him almost unquestionably dominant and elections were rare. It was in effect a 'top down' organisation, though Santamaria did not usually intervene in specific trade union work. A handful of paid organisers did most of the union work. Santamaria was mainly concerned with the 'big picture', of strategic and intellectual guidance and relationships with the Church and sometimes politicians and business. He was not at his best at lower level organising, thought by some to have an intellectual's 'tin ear' for the blue collar world.

Nobody earned a lot of money. Most of the organisers had union or industrial relations background and personalities that fitted unobtrusively into the union scene. The convention in Australia then was that union officials lived at a level reasonably close to that of their members. Most Movement organisers had union or industrial relations background and personalities that fitted unobtrusively into the union scene. Many of the ordinary members had union backgrounds of some kind too or were from established ALP families. Not a few had political ambitions. It produced some highly regarded union leaders. Not many Movement people were exotic fanatics in the way later propaganda portrayed them. Nevertheless, Cold War communists were ruthless opponents and the blood was up on both sides.

It was never clear how far Movement work was regarded as a religious obligation, but a strong sense of loyalty to the institutional Church and community prevailed. Movement members were bound by policy and if they disagreed sufficiently expected to get out. The characteristic introspective sense of Catholics being different and somewhat aggrieved tended to be heightened. A sense of Irish personal identity was common in the background, though Irish affairs as such played no part. Any criticism of the Movement tended to be seen as just part of pervasive anti-Catholicism in the public at large, and if by Catholics as disloyalty to the tribe. Santamaria kept things fairly honest; there was little of the careerism and cronyism the outside world tended to suspect. As an ardent student of the intricacies of communism – a challenge in itself in the 50s – he gave a sense of accuracy to Movement work and it avoided the sillier anti-communism of the time and the belligerent, slandering name-calling 'McCarthyism' of the US.

'Social conservatism' was still a minor issue in Australia in the 1950s. Unlike fifty or sixty years later, nearly all Australians took for granted the primacy of the traditional family and home nurturing of children. Censorship for allegedly obscene publications – which Catholic organisations generally strongly supported – was occasionally socially divisive and Movement publications sometimes grumbled about contraception. The 'liberationist' ideas of a decade later were, where they existed at all, confined to a tiny bohemian fringe. Liberal-conservative divisions in the Church were still quietly building up in the background. These were all questions for the Movement's future.

Santamaria's public jobs included, as well as National Director of Catholic Action, Director of its National Catholic Rural Movement offshoot, which was intended to develop a more 'Catholic' approach to agriculture. Its most controversial policies included much more semi-subsistence small farming and intensive settlement of immigrants on the land. People close to the land were thought to be more religiously devout and family minded, but critics saw it as implying peasant farming. Santamaria wrote voluminously on these themes but after a promising start in the 1940s, the Rural Movement faded out by the 1960s for want of support and practical objectives. By then Santamaria himself acknowledged that it was 'romantic' and not his most successful endeavour. But it made devastating propaganda against him in the Split years as the man who wanted a 'peasant on every acre'.

The (industrial) Movement advocated related 'positive policies', including much more land settlement and immigration, decentralisation, less emphasis on manufacturing development and more union-employer cooperation but these did not get much support while the anti-communist union work had priority. And they too proved decidedly unhelpful in the mid-50s.

The official ALP Industrial Groups had had a favourable press and the support of most orthodox Labor people, though later propaganda made it all seem sinister. Only a well-disposed, senior few in the unions and Party knew much about the Movement, though. Later critics often did not appreciate how shrill, vehement, ruthless and manipulative the Stalinist drive into the unions was and its rigid adherence to the 'Moscow Line'. They also over-estimated the Movement's, and particularly Santamaria's, role in what worked best as a broadly-based anti-communist effort.

The Movement's *News Weekly* magazine always seemed to see disasters awaiting the nation and guilty men thwarting attempts to prevent calamity. In the '40s the magazine had been expecting an imminent communist revolution through the unions. After 1950 it saw the threat – just as imminent – as from a takeover in Indonesia and Malaya-Singapore, backed by the Soviet Union and China. Union white-anting of the defence, even a Communist Party takeover, or perhaps invasion of Australia would then follow. Movement speakers, including priests, addressed secret meetings in churches on the 'Five Minutes to Midnight' theme, often almost luridly. Few Protestants had the same sense of urgency; indeed, it was difficult to interest Australians, even Movement sympathisers, in Asian affairs at all.

Public concern increased about Catholics moving in bigger numbers and an apparently orchestrated way into the ALP and some other public organisations. Partly this was Movement people joining the 'political party of their choice' as they were required, but they often recruited friends and relations. Groupers attracted a reputation of, like communists, talking or shouting down opponents at branch meetings and conferences, particularly over subjects like China, the Industrial Groups and the proposed ban on the Communist Party. The taunt 'commo' was thrown about when hardly deserved, but Santamaria himself developed a more subtle expression for the Labor Left – 'objectively pro-communist'. The Movement was also suspected of exerting disruptively real and imagined pressure on the Cain Labor

Government in Victoria, which won office in 1952.

The Movement took a critical turn in the early 1950s, when members and allies arrived triumphantly as delegates at ALP conferences and union assemblies after the big run of union victories. The old political enemy of hubris seemed to take over, certainly with Santamaria but with others as well. With Santamaria it might have been, too, an early, if misguided, example of the later almost entrepreneurial flair he showed for new areas of influence and support for his organisation. Santamaria began to write and speak, confidentially, about the Movement also removing from public life 'unworthy men', 'time servers' and those close to the communists. He envisaged expanding its activities into universities, the conservative parties and even business. It could 'cleanse' or 'Christianise' Australian society. These ambitions had been discussed in the Movement before and had a limited following among the clergy, but little had been done when anti-communist union work took up the available effort, other than a – controversial and uncomfortably public – Movement group at Sydney University.[‡] The new direction remained confidential and tentative, but fitted into a wider perception that the groupers had become arrogant and aggressive. Word spread – and the result was electric.

Santamaria outlined his vision for the future in a letter to Mannix at the end of 1952, when the groupers were riding high and the urgency of his anti-communist work was declining. 'Within a period of five or six years,' he wrote, 'The Social Studies Movement should be able to completely transform the leadership of the Labor Movement and introduce into Federal and State spheres large numbers of members who possess a clear realisation of what Australia demands of them and the will to carry it out ... They should be able to implement a Christian social programme ... This is the first time that such a work has become possible in Australia, and as far as I can see in the Anglo-Saxon world since the advent of Protestanism.'[§] A version of this letter became public during the Split after a visiting Indian bishop had it published in his diocesan journal – another deep embarrassment.

There could hardly have been a more sensitive nerve to hit with Protestants, one more likely to arose dormant suspicions from long past, than the threat of secretive, organised, authoritarian Catholic intervention in politics, no matter how well intentioned. Public attacks from Protestant spokesmen, mainly on the Left, increased, but the fatal reaction was from fellow Catholics and moderate union leaders. Soon the Movement had

‡ P. Morgan, *Your Most Obedient Servant*, p. 75.

§ It is comprehensively discussed in P. Morgan, B.A. Santamaria, *Running the Show*, pp. 87–189.

among its enemies the Cardinal Archbishop of Sydney, Norman Gilroy, the Premier of New South Wales, Joe Cahill, many well-placed ALP officials, and the leaders of some of the biggest 'moderate' unions in the country. Santamaria's old colleagues on the *Catholic Worker*, along with half the Catholic intellectuals in Australia, were soon discussing it critically in private and later using their pens against him on the themes of alarmism and embroiling the church in politics.

The eventual hostility to the Movement of the Sydney bishops was the greatest personal hurt of Santamaria's career. It also ended his claims to formal backing from the Church. Sydney was at best sensitive for The Movement. Gilroy did not trust Mannix's political judgment, people around him were uneasy about 'Melbourne domination' and the Archdiocese had earlier kept its distance from national Catholic Action with the similar body of its own. Early in 1954 the bishops disbanded the National Secretariat of Catholic Action in favour of independence for the dioceses and the component bodies, though because of the internal tensions rather than wider politics.

Sensitivity and misgivings turned to crisis as complaints to Gilroy and other bishops about Movement aggressiveness increased. Not politically skilled himself, Gilroy turned early in 1954 to James Carroll, a forceful and politically astute inner Sydney priest with good contacts. Gilroy placed Bishop Carroll, as he became, in charge of the Movement. Carroll began clipping the Movement's wings, while Mannix gave firm support to his protégé, Santamaria, on the ostensible grounds of protecting a lay organisation from clerical domination. Gradually over the next two years, the Church became bitterly divided and the Movement as it was disappeared.

The Split was painful for the bishops, who – to simplify – divided into two factions, headed by Melbourne and Sydney, with all the personal dislike, vituperation, factional manoeuvring and dissimulation of a big political stoush. The theoretical issue was the freedom from clerical supervision of the Movement, as a lay organisation, but the 'Sydney' faction was mainly concerned to use clerical authority to reduce the division among Catholics, and the 'sectarian' backlash and to protect the existing harmony between the Church and the Catholic-dominated New South Wales Labor Government. Sydney was determined whatever the provocation, to prevent or stifle a breakaway Labor party, as in Victoria.

The Split was also personally difficult for the Australian bishops, who abhorred division or public 'scandal' and prized the traditional order and discipline of the Church. More so than in the twenty-first century, the bishops were isolated from mainstream Australia and were looked upon with awe.

BACK O' BOURKE

B.A. Santamaria was accused of manipulating a right-wing Federal Labor faction, including the inner Melbourne MP W.M. (Bill) Bourke. Both strenuously denied the charge. 'Back o'Bourke' was a colloquial expression meaning west of Bourke, NSW – remote, near desert country.

Tanner, *Daily Telegraph*, 27 November 1954

Relations with Asia was a major issue in Australian politics in the ALP Split period. The relationship with China helped the coalition and DLP politically in the 50s and 60s but the ALP during the Vietnam War. Indonesia's expansionism added to the earlier tension when the ailing President Soekarno won control of West Papua and 'confronted' the infant Malaysian state.

Ian Gall, *Courier–Mail*, 1958

Though generally more frightened of communism than most Australians, few were politically experienced or with deep understanding of church-state theory. Often they had not taken much interest in the Movement – a youngish, semi-lay initiative anyway. Their preoccupation was with diocesan work, which included providing schools and churches for a fast growing population. They felt responsible though for the personal commitment by Movement people and the frequent career and family sacrifice involved. They usually thought of Santamaria as an 'exemplary layman' and liked him personally – he was a likeable man. Some revered him. In turn, he was always scrupulously attentive to religious detail and respectfully formal in his relations with individual bishops.

Still in his thirties, Santamaria was little known to the general public when Evatt thrust him melodramatically before the nation in October 1954. Lurid propaganda from the communists, other left-wing unions and the Australian Workers' Union soon depicted him as an exotic clerical fascist, secretly white-anting the ALP.

Santamaria was a flawed leader who succumbed to hubris in the heyday of the Groups, with the smell of power over public policy while still young and admired by bishops, clergy and many laity. Religion and politics can be an intoxicating, unstable mix, risking misjudgements due to an over-confident belief that one is doing God's work. His judgment was no doubt affected by the early admiration – reverence with some – he won from a rather closed community, swayed by his lucidity of mind and speech, his careful politeness and piety and sense of sincere and idealistic commitment

Few, though, could have brought more talents and commitment to the job. Few could argue in later decades that Australia would have been better off if the communist grip on the unions had continued unchecked. It is also difficult to see how the sustained work on the ground could have been done except through the organised Catholic community.

Though personally hurt by years of ferocious attack from the ALP, communists and hostile Catholics – and it was a very hard time too for his young family – Santamaria did not let up on the work during the crucial years after the Split when the Communist Party was partly successful in a union come-back.

Few in the Labor parliamentary parties wanted the Split. It was not seriously about ideology, though foreign affairs caused background tension and the Movement and groupers helped secure modest changes in official policy, such as softening its platform on nationalization and on opposition to government aid to non-state schools. These were in within the normal range of political debate, however, and in the end depended for implementation on voters and governments, not internal politics.

Some unofficial grouper activity did exist in in a few non-communist unions, but was a close kept secret, difficult to substantiate, fairly minor and still in its early stages. The story later was that the Movement targeted non-communist 'radical' leaders for ideological reasons. This is unlikely. It was more the decades-old tension of trade union politics, parochial but important to those involved. More often those targeted were suspect of incompetence and sometimes corruption rather than progressive.

Bob Santamaria made mistakes enough but it is hard to avoid the judgment that Evatt caused the Split, in his own bid for survival. His 1954 statement gave the internal troubles the momentum to produce devastation instead of just another nasty but manageable political party and trade union feud. There is little doubt, sadly, that he succumbed to paranoia as mental illness deepened.

Chapter 5

The Split in NSW

The Split in New South Wales, unlike in Victoria, left the ALP largely united, if bruised and it went on to win the majority of State elections for decades to come. But it was drawn-out and complicated, with a messy, rather shabby ending

Nearly every day for more than two years, news stories summarised the various often colourful manoeuvres to a perplexed public. On one side there was, as in Victoria, the 'old' executive, dominated by the newly won 'grouper' unions, such as the Ironworkers, Clerks and Miners and close to the Movement, and their supporters in the branches. It also had the support of some large, sympathetic unions, such as the State branch of the Australian Railways' Union, where ex-communist Lloyd Ross was secretary. And, unlike in Victoria, the majority of small to middling unions centred round the Labor Council (later Unions NSW) supported it; the poisonous industrial wing climate of the Melbourne Trades Hall did not exist in Sydney. These smaller unions generally preferred an alliance with the groupers rather than with the AWU or communists. Two further influential factors were traumatic memories of the disastrous cleavages in the State between the wars, when fighting of relatively minor origins developed a life of its own; and the growing Sydney-Melbourne divergence over the Church and the Movement.

The other side coalesced in the Combined ALP Unions Steering Committee, comprising about twenty-two unions, after Evatt's October 1954 attack. The left-wing unions, such as those covering the waterfront and seamen, the metal and engineering trades and miscellaneous workers, and their allies in the branches, formed one section. The otherwise 'moderate' Australian Workers' Union, its close associate, the Builders' Labourers' Federation and Barney Platt's Transport Workers' Union formed another. The General (national) Secretary of the AWU, Tom Dougherty was the dominating figure. The Steering Committee also attracted several influential people, Catholic and non-Catholic, who for various reasons were strongly anti-Movement. The corrupt elements, especially in the inner Sydney branches associated with the City Council, also mostly sided with the Steering Committee.

As Federal Parliamentary Leader, Evatt, brought the prestige of his office to the Steering Committee and it attracted the useful 'pro-Evatt' shorthand label, but Evatt's own caucus in Canberra contained many 'anti-Evatt' or 'Grouper' members, mostly Catholics. These MPs were generally supporters of Evatt's rival, the Deputy Leader, Arthur Calwell, in the sense of being ready to vote for him as against Evatt for the leadership. NSW Premier Joe Cahill and his predominantly Catholic team mostly supported the old Executive, but cautiously; they were worried about the groupers over-reaching. A State election was due early in 1956 and candidates had already been chosen. It was a situation that dictated caution. 'Out' elements (as distinct from 'ins') in Cahill's caucus supported the Steering Committee. It has to be remembered that while MPs had influence – with Cahill, a lot of it – they did not have the critical votes except as representatives of others; the organisational wing was for unions and branch members.

Much was at stake also for the challenging Left, apart from the natural desire to win and therefore dominate the State branch. Promoters of the left-wing party, with Eddie Ward as Leader, badly needed control of the NSW Branch. It was Ward's home branch and also had the biggest number of MPs, whom a left-wing executive could pressure into voting for Ward against Calwell when the time came. Less politically, many union officials wanted to be ALP members but also to work in varying degrees with members of the Communist Party – anathema to the groupers. A few were close associates of the Communist Party and sometimes even 'crypto' (secret) members, but many more were militants who were prepared, sometimes with reservations, to work alongside communists industrially. More widely, there was much sympathy throughout the ALP for more socialist policy rather than less and a more neutralist or 'independent' approach to foreign affairs.

The man at the centre of much of the storm was the Assistant State Secretary and Groups Organiser, J.T. (Jack) Kane. Kane was the chief Movement man in the ALP office, somewhat obsessive and pugnacious in his anti-communism and other pursuits, but a brilliant organiser and backroom politician. Years of exposure to the world-class intrigue of the postwar Transport Workers' Union had honed Kane's natural wiles and he was happy to turn them on as well to the frequently devious tactics of the communists. The byzantine postwar politics of the NSW branch of the Transport Workers' Union were one of the sparks that set fire to the Split nationally. Hints of corruption, factional realignments and disposable ideological allegiances were normal there. The TWU covered both owner-drivers and employed drivers, in an industry with a raffish side anyway. The particular spat in the early 1950s was Kane's allegation – he was then a truck owner-driver – that the affable State Secretary, Barney Platt, was having union cars serviced at an excessive price at a garage he (Platt) owned. Kane's campaign against Platt pushed Platt into an alliance with Tom Dougherty and the AWU and it had already brought Kane into the Movement.

Unlike many Movement people, Kane had the proletarian touch in bare-knuckle political scrapping, as a former, miner and truck driver who had had to battle in the depression. He had been a 'Lang man' in the 1930s and also flirted with the Left. A lot of union officials and parliamentarians were afraid of him.

Kane's election from this rugged background to the ALP office when the groupers won control of the NSW branch in 1952 alarmed many union leaders, regardless of ideology.

He shocked and awed colleagues with his management of the ALP end of the big campaign for the Ironworkers election in 1952, with teams of door-knocking canvassers from ALP branches and the Movement. He recruited Evatt to launch the campaign at the (Presbyterian) Assembly Hall, Movement men helping to swell the packed crowd. His success in getting an inquiry, with adverse findings, into alleged corruption in his old union (Transport Workers) and an ALP Industrial Group formed for a close-fought 'clean out' campaign there was not forgotten. Only in exceptional circumstances was an ALP Group authorised in a union under ALP control.

Doubled with Kane as a target of the Steering Committee was Frank Rooney, the Country and Northern Organiser in the ALP office. Like Kane, Rooney was a brilliant organiser, a veteran Movement man with loyalties tending to Santamaria rather than the Sydney authorities. A Newcastle man, he had largely organised the Industrial Group in the Miners union and had a leading role in the Ironworkers fight in the Hunter Valley. Moreover, by force of personality he was able to attract Protestants – often the majority of his supporters – in a way many Movement people could not. He was the chief obstacle to a Left resurgence in the Hunter Valley.

More and more it became a fight in which Dougherty wanted to drive Kane and Rooney out of their jobs. There has been much speculation about Dougherty's motivation. It is likely it was more complicated than, as Dougherty said, his wish to break Movement power in the ALP for the good of the party, after having first gone along with the Movement to assess it. It has been frequently assumed, as discussed earlier, that Dougherty feared the Groups–Movement axis would target the AWU. He also resented – and wanted revenge on – the Group-dominated State Executive because it agreed to a State Government program to reform the previously corruption-ridden Sydney City Council with proportional representation voting and a popularly elected Lord Mayor. This ended Dougherty's chance of becoming Lord Mayor, an ambition for which he had earlier allied with the groupers. There has also been speculation that corrupt elements in the ALP, often supporting the Steering Committee, had a hold over him. And there have also been other lines of speculation over the years, not often reflecting well on him.

When the delegates returned to Sydney from the Hobart Federal Conference in March 1955, Cahill's strategy was to 'play it cool', but it was an uphill battle. The Steering Committee got in first, with Evatt addressing a huge, rowdy rally called by the Port Kembla branch of the Waterside union and local ALP branches. Left strategy over the next few weeks was to organise as much public disturbance as possible, to emphasise the claims of 'outside control' and 'division', and to attract intervention from the Federal Executive. The memory of the disruptive South Coast rallies remained traumatic with NSW ALP moderate leaders for years to come.

At Cahill's request, the State Executive advanced the date of the next State Conference to April 1955, from the usual June, to 'restore unity' and in the hope – unsuccessful – of forestalling Federal intervention. Cahill by then had the support of formerly anti-grouper moderates on the Federal Executive, headed by senator Pat Kennelly, who thought things had gone too far. They negotiated a compromise where left-wingers would be given seats on the Executive, in place of militant groupers. A Special State Conference would be held as soon as possible but under Federal authority. The Federal Executive would control credentialing of delegates, but unlike in Victoria new or non-members of the ALP would not be accepted as delegates. The Federal Executive would also hear charges by Dougherty against Kane and Rooney of 'offences against the best interests of the Labor Party'. The Federal Executive would agree not to disturb pre-selections for the state election due early in 1956. Federal MPs would not be so fortunate; their pre-selections were still to be decided and some hungry eyes feasted on winnable seats.

After more talks and manoeuvring, the Special State Conference was set for 13 and 14 August. Both sides thought they could win and, unlike in Melbourne, there was no mood for boycotting it. The Left boosted its numbers compared to previous years by affiliating more unions and boosting to a maximum the number of members on which its unions were affiliated, thus giving bigger delegations. Big, rhetoric-filled public rallies proceeded the conference, with vitriolic attacks, amid much booing, on the

Movement, fascism, McCarthyism, outside control and the like on the one side; on the other tirades against 'Evattism', the 'Dougherty faction' and the communists. The left speakers roundly condemned the Victorian 'rats' and their destruction of the Cain Government and stoutly defended the 'Chifley legend'. This was the point at which 'grouper' became a dirty word, roared disdainfully from rally and conference floor. A year earlier 'grouper' had connotations of status in the party, of winning elections, but by mid-1955 it was implying a fanatical, secretly infiltrating Catholic organisation out to destroy the ALP's honour and principles.

The groupers won the day at the conference by a slither of margin from nearly 600 delegates, retaining control of the State Executive, but there were upsets and some positions went to Steering Committee candidates.

The NSW Executive right was by then dividing into militant and more moderate factions. Kane and Laurie Short of the Ironworkers headed the militants and the new State Secretary, Bill Colbourne, the moderates. Short was already under heavy pressure from the Communist Party, which could hardly believe its luck and was particularly preparing for a come-back in his Ironworkers' union, its lost prize. Abolition of the ALP Industrial Groups, as directed by the Hobart Conference, was crucial to the communist strategy. This and other threats from the far left led to the 'diehard industrial groupers', as they were dubbed, forming a new Industrial Group body, the Industrial Labor Organisation.

The Steering Committee was far from accepting defeat, but manoeuvring over Federal pre-selections for the surprise Federal election of December 1955, when Labor was so crushingly defeated, and the State election of February 1956 kept the public tension down. Labor scraped back at the February election. The Left blamed the big swing against Cahill on the State Executive and, to simplify, this helped bring another Federal intervention. Again, the Left wanted to get a more sympathetic State Executive and drive out some of the 'diehard' groupers – meaning mainly Kane and Rooney.

Some dubious tactics followed, especially allegations that a 'bodgie' ticket had helped the Right win at the special conference. The charge was that a forged 'how to vote' card had tricked some 'pro-Evatt' delegates into voting informal. A charge of grouper 'branch stacking' followed. The Federal Executive investigated and referred the conduct to another Special Federal Conference, in Melbourne in July.

The evidence for these charges was not particularly convincing and there were plausible accusations that the 'bodgie ticket' was actually printed in Dougherty's office and ineffective, and that the alleged mass recruiting into Glebe area branches was actually carried out by a prominent Dougherty supporter with inner city connections.

The Melbourne Conference was inconclusive and referred the dispute back to the Federal Executive to achieve a 'united party'. In the last, fateful intervention of the series, the Federal Executive reconstructed the State Executive for 'balance' and banned the Industrial Labor Organisation and a Movement-based Rank and File Rights Committee which had begun to campaign against the intervention. The New Executive dismissed Kane, Rooney and Alan Manning, the agnostic social democrat intellectual from *Voice* magazine, who had criticised the changes in a letter to the *Sydney Morning Herald. Voice* was an influential centrist social democratic monthly, which lost circulation and had to close down because of its 'anti-Evatt' stand. Manning had also been denouncing the 'Evatt–Chamberlain¶ dictatorship' to ALP branches and had invitations to address many more; though it was not the official reason for his expulsion, this patently non-Movement man of the centre was making it difficult to maintain the simple 'Santamaria plot' story to the rank and file.

Anger and the mood for a revolt was mounting on the Right, but the Sydney Catholic bishops called on a Movement rally of an estimated seven to eight hundred people not join a breakaway party, out of loyalty to the wishes of Cardinal Gilroy. The challenge instead was to 'stay in and fight'. The Sydney hierarchy, no less than the state parliamentarians and the others wanted to avoid at all costs a split like that in Victoria. Their failure to support the local Santamariaites and the Victorians was to cause anger and hurt among a big minority of Catholics, but subsequent voting showed that most agreed with the bishops.

Kane, Manning, well-wishers and the few who stayed with the two banned organisations, however, met on 29 September at the Sydney Trades Hall to form a new party. In a critique of the authoritarian tactics of the previous two years, they called it the Democratic Labor Party – soon known as the DLP.

¶ F.E. 'Joe' Chamberlain from Perth became Federal President in 1955.

Chapter 6
The Split in Queensland

The Brisbane Trades Hall overlooks the city centre from a hill rising behind Edward Street. Dunstan House, the headquarters of the Australian Workers' Union and in the 1950s of the Queensland Central Executive of the Australian Labor Party, was in the low lying part of the city, in Elizabeth Street. This geographical divergence put in concrete form a feud that was almost as old as the organized Labor Movement in Queensland.

The traditional and intimate alliance between the Labor Party and the AWU in Queensland reached its peak during the premiership of William Forgan Smith, a dour and autocratic Scot, from 1932 to 1942. The AWU was then led by C.G. 'Clarrie' Fallon who, in addition to being State Secretary of the AWU, was also for much of the time State President of the ALP and even for a time Federal President and State Secretary. Though respected for his strength of character and radical ideals, Fallon was nevertheless the archetypical AWU 'boss' who liked things his own way. It was said that he liked to surround himself with physically huge organizers because they would not have enough brains to oppose him; another and more likely origin given for the Queensland AWU tradition of six foot six (198 cm) organizers was that men of this stamp could persuade the most recalcitrant cane-cutter or bush worker to pay his dues.

The reasons for the AWU–ALP alliance were simple and obvious: the AWU was the biggest union in Queensland, by far. It covered not only such traditional AWU fields as the shearers, cane-cutters, metalliferous miners and other bush workers but, more than in other states, competed for membership with other unions whose organization was weak in the sprawling rural reaches.

For most State and indeed Federal parliamentarian, an alliance with the AWU was essential. For many years, the State had been organized into electoral divisions on the basis of geographically huge, lightly populated outback electorates – with their preponderance of bush workers and AWU members – returning disproportionately large numbers of State MPs because of their small populations compared to city divisions. Pre-selection was on the basis of a plebiscite among members of affiliated unions, as in Victoria; this meant that the AWU officials, with their ability to organize in the back-blocks, had tremendous influence over pre-selections. And at election time, the local apparatus of the AWU, with its paid organizers and cars, was an invaluable aid to a Labor candidate. This alliance in the field was repeated at the Labor in Politics Convention, the supreme governing body of Queensland Labor, held every three years in a different city. About 60 per cent of delegates traditionally came from unions and 40 per cent from local ALP branches, but because of the expense many outback 'branch' representatives were in fact Parliamentarians or AWU organizers. The alliance between the AWU, the political wing and a small number of 'out' other unions was easily able to control the convention. The system under which affiliated unions voted their own representatives onto the Queensland Central Executive made control of this body, supreme between conventions, more difficult, but the AWU and the political wing were still able to control it as long as they worked together.

The AWU greatly increased its hold over the ALP after the war through the Industrial Groups. As these captured other unions from communist control, the new grouper controllers tended to side with the AWU, which strongly supported the Groups. This more than made up for a tendency for the comparative strength of the AWU itself to wane, as Queensland became more industrialized.

The alliance between the AWU, the Groups and the dominant Parliamentary faction thus came to form a powerful 'right' wing of the Party in Queensland after the Second World War. It was 'right' of course only in a limited sense, since the new Premier, E.J. Hanlon, and the AWU leaders rarely hesitated to attest the usual, if qualified, faith in rhetorical socialism.

The comparatively smaller, predominantly craft unions of the Trades Hall and the 'out' factions of Parliamentarians made up the so-called 'left' wing. The main Trades Hall unions considered themselves more intellectual, more militant and more correctly orthodox than the AWU faction. A climate of folksy quasi-Marxism permeated many and not a few were under communist control. For many years the Trades and Labor Council of Queensland had a communist secretary, first Michael Healy and later Alex Macdonald. This allowed the small local Communist Party considerable, though limited, leverage on Trades Hall ideology and strategy. Ideology apart, most of the Trades Hall unions were often engaged in competition for members and working conditions with the AWU; the Trades Hall–AWU feud was in a sense bred into them. By the late 1940s, the Industrial Groups had become a convenient issue around which this deep-seated power struggle could fester.

Hanlon's Minister for Labor at this time was Vincent Clair Gair, born of a Scottish prison official father and an Irish mother at Rockhampton in 1902. Short, rotund, affable yet arrogant, devious and tenacious, Gair was the rising star of the postwar Hanlon Cabinet. He had a strong sense of Catholic anti-communism and supported the Groups warmly, yet had sufficient of the wheeler-dealer quality to be a relative favourite – for an 'in' parliamentarian – with the Trades Hall in the turbulent postwar years. He was remembered as an excellent Minister for Labour in an especially difficult time. Part of the price for this success was a degree of estrangement from the AWU leadership. Even then, the AWU leaders seemed to sense a declining role for their union in the second, more technical half of the century. Gair tended to be seen as a man less willing than an up-and-coming Queensland parliamentarian ought to be to 'toe the line' of the AWU. But by 1950, when Gair became Deputy Premier and even 1952, when Hanlon died and Gair succeeded him, this difference was a faint cloud on the horizon.

The big issue of the 1947 Labor in Politics Convention, in Townsville, was formation of the Industrial Groups. This was still an issue in Toowoomba in 1950, but it was passed in importance by a complicated faction fight, stemming from the State Parliamentary Party, in which the QCE had tried to remove the pre-selections of several parliamentarians. The Groups were a divisive issue again at Rockhampton in 1953, with eleven pro-Group and three anti-Group motions on the agenda. The right wing was easily able to control the Convention.

The State President and dominating personality of the AWU in Queensland in the first half of the 1950s was Rochus Joseph John Bukowski. A boyhood contemporary of Gair in Rockhampton, Bukowski became an AWU organiser in 1935 at Ayr, Southern Districts Secretary, stationed in Brisbane in 1942, State President in 1951 and State Secretary in 1956 upon the death of H. Boland. Although not a practicing Catholic, he was an intense anti-communist in the AWU tradition, with an almost physical hatred of communists, and he became Secretary of the Industrial Groups; in this role he worked closely with the Movement.

The Groups were part of his power base as he rose to the top of the AWU, and with it, the ALP in Queensland. He was a huge, driving – almost driven – man, given to frantically hard work and hard play. He affected to despise 'rosary bead' practicing Catholicism, yet was proud that his children were being brought up as Catholics. He was aggressively proud of the Polish name and the Polish birth of his grandparents. Many thought it part of his tragedy that he had the will to be an AWU 'boss' in the Fallon style, but possessed neither the emotional stability, the subtlety nor the time in history to do so. Men such as Tom Dougherty and Bukowski seemed to have a strong sense that they were not attaining the same unquestioned power as Fallon, the man in whose shadow they lived.

Dougherty's walk-out in Sydney in the middle of 1954 and his subsequent support of the Evatt attack on the groupers led to a grouper initiative to back Bukowski against Dougherty for the General (National) Secretary ship of the AWU. This collapsed and served only to intensify Dougherty's intransigence against the Groups. By the end of the year the whole East Coast AWU machine was behind Dougherty and after some deft manoeuvring, Bukowski was 'on side'; perhaps his position was too vulnerable, since he was feuding with the North Queensland section of the AWU, for him to afford not to be. Anyway, by the AWU Conventions of January and February 1955 he was violently attacking his erstwhile allies of the Groups and Movement in the same melodramatic exposés as his colleagues.

The Federal intervention in Victoria in late 1954 and the Hobart Conference put Gair, who declined to change sides with the AWU, onto a collision course with the big union. He had rejected its invitations to do so and attracted the implacable hostility of Dougherty. This magnified intolerably the already existing cleavage between Gair and the AWU and with Bukowski personally in Queensland.

The feud deepened steadily throughout 1955 and 1956 and an unkind Providence produced many political events to aggravate it, if ever time seemed likely to be a healer.

The political wing had sufficient strength, even without the AWU, on the Queensland Central Executive, on 25 March to defeat a motion of no-confidence in the five Queensland delegates, led by Gair, who had boycotted the Hobart Conference. But subsequently a meeting of nineteen unions affiliated to the ALP, including the AWU, voted to censure them by thirty-one to twenty-three. The State Parliamentary, however, voted its confidence in the boycotters.

From this time, the previously feuding Trades Hall unions and the AWU worked increasingly closely together, with Bukowski leading the attack on the Gair Government. A winter of discontent was followed by a Queensland Central Executive motion on 23 September recommending that the Parliamentary Party introduce the three weeks' annual leave, instead of two as agreed to by the 1953 convention. Cabinet decided, however, that the state finances would not support introduction of three weeks leave at the time and on 2 November Caucus supported this stand by a unanimous vote.

Some realignments of power brought control of the Queensland Central Executive to the Trades Hall–AWU faction by this time and it followed up the rejected 'recommendation' on annual leave a month later by 'instructing' Caucus to revoke its decision and introduce three weeks' annual leave immediately. It threatened to reconsider nominations for the 1956 elections of Labor MLAs opposing the three weeks' annual leave. Gair led the fight back against this in the Government and Caucus rejected the 'instruction' from the QCE by twenty-eight votes to twenty. The Gair Cabinet had to threaten to resign before even this narrow victory could be achieved in Caucus in the face of such a powerful threat. The stand was successful, however, and the Executive carried a motion merely asking the Government to reconsider its decision. Gair, a member of the Executive, was present and clashed heatedly with several delegates.

Though the three weeks' annual leave and other industrial issues were, in a sense, genuine, they had a greater element of symbolism. They were the sort of issues which from time to time had created tension between the political and industrial wings of Labor, but which were most inflammable when cloaking deeper power struggles.

Dougherty was making it clear in public statements at that time that he would use his great influence against Gair. He had attacked him at the 'pro-Evatt' rally in Sydney and a few weeks later virtually launched a 'Gair Must Go' slogan at an anti-Group rally with Eddie Ward in Brisbane.

Several other issues arose to aggravate the factional troubles, both in industrial relations and general state government. Queensland then had many State industrial awards, overseen by the State Industrial Court and several of its decisions upset the unions. Like much else in Queensland after forty unbroken years of Labor rule, the Industrial Court was assumed to be subject to Government influence, so the unions blamed Government influence more than they would have in the Commonwealth arbitration system. Partly the problem was changing criteria, such as 'productivity' and 'work value' in determining awards for wages. These tended to make most workers better off, but left some behind.

This situation was at its most difficult in the great shearing strike of 1956. During the wool boom years of the Korean War, the Industrial Court had awarded a 'prosperity loading' on award wages for shearers, who formed one of the biggest sections of AWU membership. By 1955 wool prices were dropping and in November the Court reduced the award rate following a claim by the United Graziers' Association for a 15 per cent reduction in the loading. The AWU had made a counter claim for a 10 per cent increase in the rate. The Court's judgment was for a 10 per cent reduction, to take effect from 1 January 1956.

The shearers, claiming that the award was a minimum, not a compulsory, rate, and that many were paid above the award, refused to work at the new rate. On 17 February, the Court declared their ban to be an unauthorized strike and issued an order restraining the AWU from encouraging its members in the ban.

The ensuing dispute threw the AWU and the Trades Hall unions more closely together than ever. Without this support, the AWU would not have been able to fight the issue through. It was a momentously emotional one for the AWU and indeed the Labor Movement generally, for a shearers' strike in Queensland against reduced wages had led to the formation of the Labor Movement in its modern form in the 1890s.

The AWU declared wool shorn at the new rate 'black'. Many shearers, often from interstate, broke the union ban to shear at the new rate as the season opened in the North, and the railway unions refused to carry the 'black' wool. Graziers started carrying it to Brisbane by road. In Brisbane, the Storemen and Packers', Transport Workers' and Waterside Workers' unions refused to handle the wool and the April wool sales were cancelled. The United Graziers' Association applied successfully to the Court in July for the clause in the award granting preference in employment to unionists to be struck out.

The Gair Government was in an appalling dilemma. It was under pressure from the unions which controlled it to assist in an intensely emotional, bitterly fought dispute. Yet wool was vital to the Queensland and Australian economies. The Queensland Railways were losing £100,000 a month. Wool was piling up in stores and often on the sheep's overloaded back.

The climax came when the September sales had to be cancelled. The Government's attitude had been that it could not interfere in the jurisdiction of the Industrial Court. Now, ten months after the controversial award, it approached the (coalition) Federal Government and both agreed to take whatever steps were necessary to ensure that the 'black' wool would be shipped. A special sale was scheduled for 1 to 4 October.

Dougherty declared in Sydney on 7 September that Gair would go down as 'the only Labor Premier in history who has openly consorted with an anti-Labor Prime Minister [Sir Arthur Fadden was Acting Prime Minister at the time] and asked an anti-Labor Federal Government to put troops in charge of the Brisbane wharves.' Both he and Bukowski accused Gair of disloyalty to the Labor Movement.

Gair replied that his government had a grave responsibility to see that the economy of the state and the welfare of its people were protected. The strike lasted for most of the year, with wool declared 'black', failed conferences and negotiations, including by the Government, with other unions involved and an atmosphere of great bitterness. It ended only in December, with the Industrial Court reinstating preference for unions as from January 1957.

The 1956 Labor in Politics Convention opened in Mackay on 28 February in the militant atmosphere of the early shearing strike. The AWU and the Trades Hall, reversing most of previous history, acted together as a broad industrial wing. They controlled the Convention and several prominent politicians subsequently lost pre-selection.

Annual leave became the great symbolic issue of the Convention. J.P. Devereux of the Amalgamated Engineering Union – ironically, a former grouper and State President of the Movement – moved that the Conciliation and Arbitration Act be amended to provide for three weeks' annual leave, with four weeks for shift workers. This motion did not specific a date for the expanded leave to apply; but then V.T. Hefferan of the Shop Assistants' Union, moved an amendment that the Act be amended in 1956 and take effect from 1 January 1957.

The outnumbered political wing, while not opposing the principle vehemently opposed the move to direct them on timing. It introduced a completely new principle into relations between the industrial and political wings, they said.

Gair said that never before had a Convention presumed to direct a Labor Government on the timing of implementation of a policy decision. He said the move conflicted with the ALP Platform stipulation on 'constitutional utilisation' of government machinery. It would be fatal politically for the Government to accept a direction in timing, he said.

'Parliament would not be a supreme body if its members were subjected to outside coercion, intimidation or direction,' he said. 'You cannot have responsible government once the decisions of any party in parliament become subject to a review by an outside body other than the electorate.'

Jack Egerton (Boilermakers' Society), Secretary of the Metal Trades Federation, Vice – President of the Trades and Labor Council and a rising figure on the Left (he later became full-time President of the Trades and Labor Council and ALP State President) put the militant view. Egerton said:

'I think there is much logic in what the Premier said, but the time for logic has disappeared. The Labor Party said that the time for logic was three years ago … The Premier can have his Constitution and the Premier can have his Premiership and we will not presume to direct the Government. But we will presume-and only because it is forced upon us – to direct the parliamentary representatives of the Australian Labor Party.'

Cabinet held an emergency meeting that night, 29 February, and the press reported that Gair had threatened to resign as Premier. There was limited enthusiasm in Cabinet and – according to the press – in the industrial wing for a split, however.

Press reports said a compromise was being reached, but next day Gair told the Convention that Cabinet did not accept the resolution. He said the direction was contrary to the rule of constitutional government and a negation of the principle of responsible democratic government, namely, that the Government was responsible to the electors and only to the electors.

Gair delivered his policy speech for the normally due State election on 24 April, devoting most of his seventy-three-minute speech to an account of the Government's record. He did not mention the three weeks leave.

Despite the turmoil over this issue and the drawn-out shearers' strike, Labor was returned with a sweeping victory on 19 May. It held all its 1953 gains. A probable reason for its popularity was the 'little horror' Budget introduced by Menzies in the Federal Parliament a few weeks earlier; amongst other things this had increased the tax on beer. Other reasons probably included an unimpressive State Opposition and, according to some commentators, popular approval of Gair's 'standing up' to the unions.

The recession of mid-1956 strengthened Gair's economic arguments against extra annual leave. He insisted that a Labor Government could not give extra annual leave if it would mean dismissal of State employees.

During the controversy, the predominantly right wing 'white-collar' and State Service unions had sought an extra week's leave for members already getting three weeks and the overall campaign had developed into one for an extra week's leave for all. Apart from the argument about shortage of State funds, Gair claimed that Queensland would not be able to attract the manufacturing industry it badly needed if it required longer annual leave than other states.

By September, the Queensland General Executive was mounting its own counter-battle of tactics. It wrote to all Labor MLAs asking them whether they were prepared to vote for the introduction of three weeks leave in 1956, but the Parliamentary Party again voted against introduction of the legislation, twenty-eight to nineteen.

One other event with major implications for internal Labor politics in 1956 was the Lands Royal Commission. In 1955 and early 1956, the AWU paper the *Worker* had run a campaign alleging maladministration and hinting at scandal in the Lands Department. The Queensland Country Party senator Ian Wood alleged in the Senate that some graziers had been forced to pay large sums of money to obtain renewals for their leases (Much Queensland grazing land was leased from the state). Gair announced a Royal Commission of Inquiry. The Minister for Lands, T.A. Foley, was relieved of his portfolio at his own request. Foley denied that he had, as alleged, sought £1,000 from a grazier, F.M. Bell, for party funds in return for favourable consideration. Foley was expelled from the ALP.

Several other controversies further poisoned the air. In a separate dispute another member was expelled for publicly attacking the Central Executive for 'bulldozing decisions'. In the 'dim sim petrol' affair, the Government agreed to import petrol from Taiwan to compete with the major oil companies. The majors had been refused the price increase they sought when the world oil price soared during the Suez Canal crisis of late 1956. In retaliation, they stopped sending standard grade fuel to Queensland. The Government then demanded that the majors' service station add another pump for the imported fuel. Stories circulated alleging corruption, including one oil major offering a large sum to have enabling legislation dropped. There was a respectable viewpoint, however, that the plan was too impetuous and draconian and could damage an essential industry rather than help the buying public. In the end the Government split and the 'dim sim petrol' plan lapsed.

Three weeks' annual leave was still a burning issue when the climactic year of 1957 opened. Apart from the issue involved, pride, principle and political advantage were – as it happened, irreversibly – aroused on both sides. For the AWU, half a century's domination of Queensland politics was at stake. The idea of the industrial wing directing soft, self-seeking politicians to implement radical industrial measures was deeply ingrained in many of the militant left – as was the fear of the Left being returned to its relative impotence if the AWU and politicians got together again. Whatever Macdonald's personal inclinations as a responsible Trades Hall leader, the Communist Party had no love for Labor Governments and had a vital interest in maintaining a toehold in Queensland Labor as a shield for its foothold in Victoria; the communist 'line' at this time is believed to have been that Gair should be manoeuvred into resignation. For Gair and his Government, economics aside, the principle of reasonable freedom from machine dictation was vital; if it gave in on this, other demands could be expected. 'QCE dictation' was a longstanding allegation from the Opposition, which could affect votes.

Bitter exchanges illustrated the increasingly unpleasant turn that personal animosities were giving the issue. Gair's personal contempt, never well concealed, for Bukowski as a bully was now obvious. Bukowski, who is remembered as having become rather rattled and distorted in judgment under the stress of the Split years, retaliated with a burning hatred of Gair, who was capable of arrogance and lack of tact in his personal relations.

On 28 February, the Queensland Central Executive issued an ultimatum to State Labor Parliamentarians on the three weeks leave issue. By fifty-two votes to eleven, it warned members that opposition to legislation for three weeks leave would be dealt with by the Executive 'in accordance with the Party's rules'.

A 5 April conference on annual leave ended with yet further failure to agree and on 10 April Gair had said adamantly: 'I favour three weeks' annual leave when Queensland can afford it – not when the Queensland Central Executive tells me to do it. Because of lack of money we have had to sack 2,000 men from Government employ. Three weeks leave would cost at least £400,000 a year – probably £1,250,000 when its implication are fully worked out. To introduce it we would have to sack more men. I won't do it.'

On 18 April the Queensland Central Executive carried by thirty-five votes to twenty-seven a motion declaring that the Premier no longer had the confidence of the Labor Movement. It called on him to attend a special meeting to show cause why he could not be expelled from the ALP. The lengthy motion accused Gair of 'continued and openly expressed defiance of Convention and the Executive.'

The dénouement of two and a half years of internal strife was set for 24 April. The Premier, a tubby, jaunty, gutsy little figure in a bow tie and felt hat, entered the lift at Dunstan House in the late afternoon of that day and rode in a lift to the seventh floor to meet his executioners.

He had behind him a declaration from his Cabinet the day before, declaring its confidence in him and carrying the signed promise of each minister except Jack Duggan, his deputy and rival, to stick with him.

The issue then went to Caucus and after nearly six hours' debate, the members voted twenty-six to twenty-one to give the Premier unqualified support, declaring that Gair had at all times scrupulously carried out the decisions of Caucus.

The Gair affair had attracted publicity throughout Australia and far beyond; it even earned an editorial in the London *Times*. The weight of comment was overwhelmingly on the side of Gair, as the elected leader of a sovereign government refusing dictation by an outside machine. His position was also attracting attention from the Movement, the DLP and the Anti-Communist Labor Party, which began preliminary organization in Queensland. They already had a core of support in some unions, most notably the Clerks' and State Service unions, and the allure of attracting a seemingly wronged Premier and Cabinet to the cause was obvious.

Gair now faced six detailed charges, laid by both judge and jury. They began with defiance of the Labor-in-Politics convention and extended to his handling of recent controversial issues, including petrol and land leasing.

Gair had been a member of the ALP since 1919 and of the Parliament since 1932. His parents had been members of the Party since almost the turn of the century. Faced with the end of this tradition, he spoke emotionally, his eloquence sometimes disintegrating into choked groping for words.

There was no offence alleged against him, he told the Executive, which could be attributed solely and exclusively to any action of his. Therefore, it was really a trial of the Cabinet and Caucus. It was a trial of every individual member of both bodies. It was the trial of every individual member of both bodies. It was the trial of men who had given a lifetime of service to the Labor Movement and who had been privileged finally to represent it in Parliament. He said the history of the Party showed there had been differences between the Executive and the Parliamentary Party on many occasions. The indefensible publicity in the daily press exposing their differences, exaggerating their dissension, had fanned a difference into what could easily be a disaster.

The historic motion read:

'This Executive, after hearing Mr Gair state his case in showing cause why he should not be expelled from the Australian Labor Party, decides that he has not refuted the charge that he has defied Convention's decision on the matter of three weeks leave, and that he has not shown that he has not repudiated his personal pledge in the matter of three weeks leave, given to a number of delegates.'

The Queensland Split was not especially about the Movement, which had worked unobtrusively in the State for a decade under the AWU wing and made few enemies. But the southern troubles created, as Gair said, the 'climate of the times', of suspicion, over-reaching and stubbornness. Tom Dougherty's war against the Movement was a dominant factor in creating this 'climate'. His influence was weakening, however, and along with it AWU cohesion; two of the AWU's QCE representatives had voted against Gair's expulsion. Evatt and other southern leaders had also tried, too little and too late, to stop the Queensland Split.

Gair called his Parliamentary supporters together on 26 April. Eight ministers were present and the Treasurer, Ted Walsh, gave his support from Bundaberg. Twelve rank and file members of the Parliamentary Party and some other supporters officially banded together that day as the Queensland Labor Party. The meeting appointed a committee of five to frame a constitution and rules. Gair announced that the Queensland Labor Party would not affiliate with the Democratic Labor Party. Gair's rival, Jack Duggan, resigned as Minister for Transport and the remaining Parliamentary Labor Party appointed him Leader.

Frank Nicklin, the (Country Party) Leader of the Opposition, announced that the Opposition would not 'carry' the Gair Government and denied suggestions of a 'deal' by which Gair would be supported for some time in exchange for a revision of electoral boundaries and legislation for compulsory court-controlled ballots – a threat believed to terrify the AWU leadership.

The next weeks were bitter with public recrimination between the two Labor parties, with savage personal attacks between Duggan and Gair revealing the depth of their mutual personal antagonism. Senator Condon Byrne, a barrister who had once been private secretary to Gair, resigned from the ALP and joined the two ALP (Anti-Communist) senators, McManus and Cole, on the cross-benches in Canberra. Labor Party branches and regional bodies began to split throughout the state as the Queensland Labor Party spread from its parliamentary nucleus.

Resumpton of Parliament in June, brought two days of perhaps the bitterest and angriest debate the jacaranda-shaded sandstone building beside the Brisbane River had ever known.

Duggan called Gair a 'little dictator' and vehemently denied that personal ambition to succeed Gair had motivated his actions. Hostile interjections from the QLP and Opposition benches flew throughout his speech. Gair said many MPs now supporting Duggan had changed their stance when 'Big boss Joe and others started to wield their whips'.

On 12 June a motion to grant supply was defeated by 45 votes to 25. The ALP and the two Opposition parties voted together and the Gair Government fell. A new election followed on 3 August.

The Queensland Split had less sectarian bitterness than that in Victoria. There were many Catholics on both sides (including Gair, Bukowski and Duggan) and several Protestants in the QLP. In most dioceses, the Church remained neutral and the Movement, smaller in Queensland anyway, was hardly an issue, though the sectarian flavour of the national Split generally had affected Queensland.

Evatt, Calwell, Ward and Cain from Victoria were among the Southern leaders who campaigned for the ALP and there were press reports that Evatt was less than welcome. Bukowski told the press the Queensland Central Executive had not asked Evatt to take part in the campaign, but the Trades Hall unions gave him an enthusiastic welcome.

Many seem to have felt deep down during the first half of 1957 that labor could not really be defeated in Queensland. It had been there too long; the seats were too favourably distributed; the Liberals and the Country Party were too weak. All that had to happen was for the truculent Gair to go and be replaced by the more co-operative Duggan.

Labor had governed in Queensland continuously for twenty-five years and, with the exception of the 1929–32 period, since 1915 – since before most of the participants in the 1957 Split could remember. Now, in a changing society, the rural bias in seat distribution which had once favoured Labor rebounded.

The Country Party won eight seats to gain a total of twenty-four in the new Assembly and the Liberals added ten for a total of eighteen. The ALP obtained twenty seats and the QLP eleven, both Labor parties together thus being outnumbered by the combined opposition parties.

When the new Parliament met on 27 August, the first non-Labor Gove for a quarter of a century sat on the Treasury benches, with Nicklin as Premier, to be followed a decade later by Joh Bjelke-Petersen.

Chapter 7
The Rise of Whitlam

Expulsion from the ALP of Premier Gair was the last big event of the Split, but the legacy lasted for fifteen years. The Democratic Labor Party in NSW joined up with the ALP (Anti-Communist) in Victoria in 1957 to form the nucleus of a national DLP. The Movement gave it the basis for a modest presence in the other states. Gair's Queensland Labor Party merged into the DLP in 1962. The DLP attracted new members in most states, some of whom saw it has the basis for a new 'centre party' without union control, others as an expression of strong anti-communist or Catholic feelings. Like other smaller parties since, much of its vote was a 'protest' vote, since with both Labor and the Liberals there was usually much to protest about.

Following the practice begun in Victoria in 1955, the DLP gave its preferences to the Liberals and estimated that 90 per cent of DLP voters followed the how-to-vote card. It was reckoned that about two-thirds of the DLP vote would have gone to the ALP before the Split. DLP strategy was to keep Labor out of office until it agreed to a rapprochement. At least half the Catholics in Victoria voted DLP. The DLP usually got about 15 per cent of the total vote in Victoria and about 10 per cent in Queensland, varying with candidate and issue, and up to 5 per cent in other states. Its best votes were for strong candidates for the Senate. This voting pattern took away nationally at least 5 per cent of the vote that would normally have gone to Labor, a huge obstacle to it returning to office.

The DLP claimed a membership of 14,000 in Victoria, but active membership was more like 3,000. Queensland may have had half as many and the other states 1000 or fewer members. In 1958 it lost the one Victorian Legislative Assembly seat it won in 1955, but it was able to win enough Senate seats to hold the balance of power in Canberra for most of the time from 1955 to 1974. It usually supported the coalition governments. Frank McManus, former Assistant Secretary of the ALP in Victoria, was a DLP senator from 1955–62 and 1965–74 and Queensland's Vincent Gair – who was chosen as Leader – from 1965–74. Jack Kane, the former NSW Assistant

Secretary of the ALP, became Federal Secretary of the DLP and a major raiser of funds from business to finance a national organisation, though its vote and membership were small outside Victoria and Queensland. Kane's fund-raising and, much more, grateful help from Liberal coffers financed the DLP's theatrically anti-Labor election campaigns. Kane won a surprise fifth Senate seat for the DLP in NSW in 1970, during a period of internal turmoil in both the ALP and the coalition.

The DLP attacked Labor for alleged communist control behind the scenes and for its policies on foreign affairs and defence – areas where Labor's natural instinct was to veer towards defence neutralism and anti-militarism, trends strengthened by the left-wing unions and the varying degrees of communist influence in them. In this and many other ways the DLP was the political arm of the Movement. Nevertheless, it was not a happy arrangement. Inside the DLP Santamaria's efforts at control from outside, or speaking publicly on its behalf when he was not a member were often deeply resented. There was acrimonious rivalry for financial support. As early as 1959 Stan Keon and Bill Bourke, two of the MPs driven out of the ALP as alleged Movement infiltrators, publicly attacked Santamaria over control and withdrew from active politics. Many who were attracted in the hope of the DLP becoming a progressive centre party also dropped away. DLP domestic policies never amounted to much and often gave the impression of grab-bag thrown together to please various supporters, but they emphasised Movement favourites such as decentralisation, profit sharing and cooperatives and a voucher system for state aid to non-government schools. As with ALP Left policies, these remained on the margin of public discussion and created little interest, even among their own supporters, especially as the DLP had no hope of winning office in its own right. Despite its best attempts not to be, it was usually thought of as a 'church party', suspect as covertly against contraception and the like. Another problem was the seeming harsh and unattractive shrillness and exaggeration of its anti-communism, and of its attacks on the ALP and 'Evattism', especially at election time. At the crucial 1963 Federal election – coming after the ALP had almost won in 1961 – the DLP showed piles of human skulls in its TV advertisements, as symbolic of the communism which was supposedly dominating the ALP. The skulls were those or Polish officers, killed by Russians in World War II.

The DLP gave the impression, with some accuracy, of being a very angry party. This reflected, in Victoria at least, some also very angry Catholic parishes, outraged not only at the return to influence of the Communist Party but even more the expulsion and thus defeat of many Catholic MPs, a huge insult to the tribe. Some parishes were bitterly divided, for and against Catholic politicians like Arthur Calwell, who stayed with the ALP. While angry sermons flowed from many a Catholic pulpit, some also flowed from Protestant ones protesting against Catholic Action. Accuracy was not always present on either side.

An exception to the generalisation above about domestic policy was DLP support for State Aid to independent and Catholic schools. DLP policy – and Movement and grouper policy before it – was one among several factors that brought the beginnings of State Aid in 1963, when the Menzies Government announced at election time Federal funds for school science laboratories. This broke the century-old dam wall of resistance and soon coalition and, warily, some state governments, Labor as well as coalition, were granting limited assistance. Labor federal policy remained adamantly hostile, though how far this was out of conviction and how far to distance itself from the hated DLP and its own right-wing is difficult to know. It was an especially sensitive subject at the time, as the postwar baby and immigration boom was crowding Catholic schools particularly, when at the same time recruiting for the orders of nuns and brothers was plummeting.

The Movement meanwhile ceased to exist. In 1957 the rival groups of bishops took its disputed status to Rome. The pro-Santamaria bishops wanted it to be a Catholic Action body, formally linked to the Church but independently operated by laymen. The Sydney-led group wanted it to be firmly under the bishops. The Vatican would not allow either policy for an organisation that seemed too close to a political party and ordered that it become wholly independent of the Church. In 1958 the Sydney bishops quietly closed the fraying Movement down, though allowing a low-key educational and industrial body to continue. The Santamaria Movement became the National Civic Council, Catholic-based but independent of the Church and national in scope. Favourable Church sources still helped with the funding, but it had to seek more outside money and cut its costs. The NCC was anything but secretive, except in its rather closeted union role.

The divisive foreign affairs issues turned to Indonesia in the '60s, as the Malaysian problems gradually settled. Indonesian President Sukarno, hero of the postwar independence struggle, was an indifferent peacetime administrator and his position had become shaky. As more conventional supporters lost confidence in him, to hold office Sukarno relied more and more on the large Indonesian Communist Party. He also turned to expansionism, claiming – and obtaining – West Papua for Indonesia. With less success, he also claimed part of the island of Borneo that was being incorporated into Malaysia and began an abortive 'confrontation', partly bluster but with a small military content. A further concern was that when the ageing Sukarno fell, the Communist Party would take over, with perhaps a civil war, more aggressive expansion in the neighbourhood or support for revolution elsewhere in Asia, much as China and the Soviet Union in theory did. While Maoist China belligerently preached support for 'wars of liberation', in practice it did little; it was itself mired in the weakness of the 'Great Leap Forward' and 'Cultural Revolution'. The Moscow–Peking split did not necessarily ease the Cold War, as there was a fear that each might try to outdo the other – and that Indonesia might add its efforts.

These developments were, politically, ready-made for both Menzies and the DLP, for unswerving support for the US and Britain as bedrock defence and foreign affairs policy. It was the scenario that led to Menzies introducing conscription of 20-year-olds for military service in 1964 and the following year increasing the Australian commitment, including conscripts, to the war in Vietnam from a small advisory unit to fighting men. It was not so easy for Labor, divided as so often between a conventional foreign affairs approach and a neutralist or isolationist Left. The final years of the decade began to work for Labor, however, as public opposition to conscription and the Vietnam commitment deepened. Then 1971 brought a lucky break, when future Prime Minister Gough Whitlam led a Labor delegation to Beijing, promising recognition, just as China was opening to the world and President Richard Nixon announced that he would visit there.

Foreign affairs apart, the ALP, as well as having the DLP as a roadblock, was its own worst enemy. Caucus retained Evatt as leader – and thus alternative prime minister – until 1960. There was an element of sentiment in sticking with an embattled leader, but at first the chief reason for his survival was pressure on caucus members from the left-wing unions and the AWU. The Left had no time for Evatt, but wanted to keep Calwell out until it had amassed the 'numbers' for Ward. Evatt provided his usual election extravaganza in 1958 by suddenly, in mid-campaign, offering to stand down as Leader if the bitterly hostile DLP would give its preferences to the ALP. The DLP quickly rejected the offer; its sights were on the left-wing union control in Victoria and Queensland and the foreign affairs policies. But it would have been decidedly odd for Labor, seeking national government, to go to the polls without a leader.

Ward finally challenged for the leadership on 16 February 1959, but Evatt defeated him by 46 votes to 32, with the Right supporting Evatt this time. A reluctant Evatt finally went the following year when the NSW machine arranged for him to be appointed Chief Justice of the NSW Supreme Court, though the State Government was uneasy. (Joe Cahill died in 1959 and Robert Heffron was Premier.) Evatt's mental confusion became obvious on the bench until he collapsed in 1962 and remained unconscious until he died in 1965.

By 1960 a new force had taken over in NSW – the AWU has ended its fling with the Left and formed with the existing right a new 'NSW Right' which was to be the backbone of the ALP for half a century – not always lovely but very effective. Wags joked that it was the 'grippers and groupers'. (Masons and Catholics, which had a tad of truth.) The AWU district branches were by then exercising relatively more power and the General (National) Secretary, Dougherty, less than he had accrued in the mid-50s. The avuncular NSW AWU State secretary, Charlie Oliver – who had once 'carried the swag' in the outback with a young Joe Chamberlain – became a power in the new force.

Calwell at last had the 'numbers' and was elected Leader on 7 March 1960, but the drama was in the choice of his deputy. The NSW Right backed the elegant, articulate young Sydney barrister Gough Whitlam, who now defeated Ward on the final ballot by 38 votes to 34. This was a contest Ward and his backers expected to win and it would have kept him in the race for the medium term. Ward was memorably shattered and angry. He finally congratulated Whitlam but some months later in another dispute he punched at Whitlam, an even bigger and much younger man, at 43 and six feet 4 inches (193 cm).[**]

The ALP had high hopes for Calwell, as an established public figure and prominent Catholic identified with the Party's right. Calwell was at last also lucky. With an election due late in 1961, the economy slumped into a nasty recession and unemployment doubled to 4 per cent, after a heavy-handed Canberra 'credit crunch'. Calwell campaigned on a platform of renewed economic expansion and Labor got to within one seat of beating Menzies. The obvious – and easiest – political course, with the sides so balanced, was for Calwell to 'not rock the boat', to at all costs avoid public trouble and division. The 'steady as it goes' strategy lasted for two years, until Menzies secured an election for 30 November 1963, on the grounds that the Government needed a more secure majority than 62 votes to 60 in the House of Representatives. Sadly, for Calwell, the voters ceased their flirtation with Labor and returned to the pattern of 1955 and 1958, with the ALP down to 45 per cent of the vote, compared to 48 per cent two years earlier.

** Ross McMullin, The Light On the Hill, pp. 289–91; E. Spratt, *Eddie Ward, Firebrand of East Sydney*, p. 249.

A new era of memorable turmoil then set in for the ALP, as it seemed that office could not be won without drastic change. However, like Evatt before him, Calwell clung to the leadership, at 68 years of age and after successive election defeats. To secure his position, he moved to the left, joining the Victorian Central Executive, which the far left dominated. The VCE controlled his pre-selection, as it had the pre-selections of all the State's parliamentarians since the Split. The vulnerability of his pre-selection had long been seen as a factor, apart from personal courage and disposition, in Calwell's rather acquiescent approach to critical issues in the previous ten years.

Many ALP people, in and out of the caucus, were furious at Calwell, both for thwarting Whitlam's day by staying on and for his switch to a factional allegiance he had once conspicuously opposed. His age also increasingly showed in a more cantankerous, vitriolic public style. He displayed a hatred for Santamaria and the DLP, but less publicly also for Whitlam, his likely successor. Whitlam began to strike out independently, developing more of his own public profile. He stressed that the main purpose of the ALP was to win office federally and that it could be achieved by making the party more attractive to voters. He made party reform his cause.

A sensitive issue for the ALP in the lead-up to the 1963 election had been a Government proposal to allow an American defence base at Exmouth Gulf on the Northwest Cape, to be part of a global network for controlling submarines carrying the Polaris nuclear missile - anathema to the Left. Calwell had made a practice, as Evatt had, of using the Federal bodies to shore up his own leadership, where stronger leaders would have referred much less to the organisational wing. He had called a Special Federal Conference for March 1963 to decide on the NW Cape base and other foreign policy issues. Calwell's compromise position, which the conference supported by a narrow margin, was that the base was acceptable ALP policy if Australia had joint control. The Americans were unenthusiastic about joint control, but there was a more immediate problem. Inadvertently, the conference gave rise to the 'faceless men' tag, to be used so often against Labor in the years to come. The Sydney *Daily Telegraph* journalist Alan Reid ('The Red Fox'), the most perceptive writer on Labor's internal struggles, organised a photographer to capture Calwell and Whitlam waiting - as it happened by chance - under street lights outside the Kingston Hotel in Canberra for the conference to decide Labor's stance on the base. The Liberals used this opportune picture to dramatize a charge that '36 faceless men' (mostly union officials) decided Calwell's policy on a crucial national security question, while the aspiring

Prime Minister waited out on the street. It was probably a factor in Labor's election setback later that year.

Whitlam used this incident as the trigger for a campaign during the next few years to get representation for parliamentarians on both the Federal Executive and Conference and for a generally wider basis for a Federal Conference, open to the public. More privately, he also planned to use these bodies much less than his two predecessors, restoring more power to the parliamentarians. Major public issues, particularly state aid and non-white immigration, were also on his agenda. Partly at his instigation the 1965 Federal Conference began softening Labor's rigid adherence to the 'White Australia' immigration policy and its Federal opposition to state aid. He proposed a 'needs basis' for state aid, which would have directed government to the poorer Catholic schools rather than independent colleges. He pushed these issues much harder – and eventually successfully – after he became Leader in 1967 when Calwell finally retired. The 1969 Federal Conference was the first open to the press and public and included, as well as the six delegates from each state, the four Commonwealth parliamentary leaders and the parliamentary leaders from each state. These conferences in the late 1960s changed Labor policy on the stubborn White Australia immigration and State Aid issues.

Death had a big role in the mid-60s. Ward died suddenly, of a heart attack, in mid-1963, aged 64. In November Archbishop Mannix, Santamaria's principal episcopal supporter, died, at 99 still in office. And then in March 1964 Vic Stout died, also still in office as Secretary of the Victorian Trades Hall Council, though nearing 80. He had held the industrial wing together since the early 1950s.

Ward's death brought the end of what remained of that stage of the 'socialism now' plan for a left-wing party. Much of this strategy has been based on the old Marxist idea of a 'collapse of capitalism' in a crisis. In the 1960s, pessimists, both on the left and right, still believed the 1930s depression would return. This idea was based more on anti-business prejudice and instinct than on sober forecast, but the quick return to prosperity after the 1961 slump showed what was already obvious, that capitalism was usually winning out, world-wide, against the ever sorrier looking socialism of any kind. Clyde Cameron's vision had been of Ward bringing the Left to radical power with great thumping public speeches during an economic crisis. Now it was not to be. This fading vision looked a lot like the 'Langism' that had brought young Eddie Ward into Parliament in 1931.

Socialist ideas being considered in the early 1960s – though hardly ever developed with detailed thought – included stringent economic planning and establishment of government-owned enterprises to compete with private sector 'monopolies'. As with some of Santamaria's ideas, these attracted little interest outside the Labor Movement. They were almost the opposite of conventional thinking for the economy – that Australian business often needed to become bigger in scale so as to be more efficient and globally competitive and that central economic planning would just would not work. Predictably, the most pronounced 'socialist' policies came from the Victorian conferences soon after the Split, but the Federal conferences watered them down to nebulous statements of good intent. Little more was heard of specific socialist proposals.

Ideas that made more sense in the 1930s were still alive and well in the ALP in the 1960s, nevertheless. 'Big government', as they would soon be dubbed, policies were attractive to the ALP Right as well as to the Left, as was a more 'independent' foreign policy. The essential difference was that the Right was prepared to seek government with more moderate policies until the voters were ready for big change; the Left envisaged precipitous change in more cataclysmic conditions.

The Left chose as it new leader Dr Jim Cairns, a Melbourne University economic history lecturer and former policeman who had defeated Stan Keon in Yarra in1955. With blond, clean cut features, searching blue eyes, crisply articulate speech and seemingly penetrating sincerity, Cairns created much excitement in a politically jaded community. To some he was the man of the hour, the intellectual of conscience, vision and real principle who would rejuvenate and unite Labor from the Left; to others a dangerous 'pink' radical, suspiciously close to the Communist Party. To some who knew him better, he was a well-intentioned dreamer, presentable but lacking in judgment and easily led. His most publicly eminent time was as a spokesman against Australian participation in the war in Vietnam and leader of the huge 'moratorium' street marches and other demonstrations against it. Though in practice ineffectual, he seemed to readily attract supporters to push him forward and he became Deputy Prime Minister for a short time in the mid-70s.

For the fifteen years it controlled the Labor organisational wing, the Left in practice was more concerned with heresy hunting than serious policies for government. Joe Chamberlain (Federal President 1955–61) spelled this out in his presidential address to the 1957 Federal Conference. He added the groupers to the long list of historic Labor enemies, such as capitalists, bankers, employers and the press: 'We are beset on many sides by our enemies,' Chamberlain told the 36 delegates meeting in private. 'Not only do we continue to face the traditional enemy of conservatism, supported by a powerful daily press, we face, too, the fanatical hostility of those who were defeated at Hobart ... They have not laid down their arms ... Do not underrate this enemy ... The evidence is clear that they have not given up the struggle to control the policies of this party ... not all of them have left the Labor Party ... It is part of the plan to have many of them remain within ...'[††]

This speech sums up the overall direction of the Party for the next decade and a half, what can best be described as Labor fundamentalism: firm industrial wing control, much talk (though negligible real action) about socialism and principles, obsessive loathing of the groupers, inside and out of the party, along with all the older enemies.

What made Chamberlain, the chief organisational figure of the period, tick? The many theories include vague rumours about earlier links with the Communist Party and being yet another of the, as it would later be put, authoritarian control freaks of the time. What is clear, though, is that his policies maintained not only his own position as the 'king-maker' but relative peace in a lot of Australian trades halls, especially his own in Perth. He kept out the groupers but also kept the communist resurgence under control through 'unity tickets' in union elections. These were 'how to vote' cards and other material for union elections in which ALP members could stand together as a team with communists or members of other parties. The Victorians and the far left wanted them, while NSW and the AWU-dominated right opposed them and the Federal bodies banned them. Chamberlain's apparent strategy was to not enforce the Federal ban, so that he could hold the support of those to his left, while not giving the Communist Party many new opportunities – especially in his own Western Australia. The strategy kept the communists 'on tap but not on top'.

While they were dog days for the ALP, it was actually a golden age for trade unionism. Union membership was growing rapidly with the population and economy. More than half the employed workforce belonged to unions, compared with more like a fifth half a century later. Protected manufacturing, along with economic and productivity growth was allowing steady and substantial wage increases through arbitration. The financial weakness and fragmentation of the unions in earlier times had been overcome, but the individual unions were still small and specialised enough to be close to their members. Union officials usually lived modestly and there were few scandals. White-collar unions, too, were growing fast and working more often with the blue collars, though still organisationally apart. Much of the tension of

††R. Murray, *The Split, Australian Labor in the Fifties*, p. 332.

the Cold War years had passed. With declining membership and conviction, the communists were less belligerent than a few years earlier, the Groups had gone and the NCC worked quietly, often clandestinely, mainly towards the white-collar end. There the NCC challenged new era Marxists, who without organised opponents might have become dominant. Industrially, there was no big ideological gulf between left and right, though the left unions were readier to strike and demonstrate. From a union office viewpoint, one big benefit was that there was less competition, and thus fewer elections, for union positions than before 1955.

There were several attempts at rapprochement with the DLP but it was virtually impossible. The left-wing unions adamantly opposed it and the right-wing ones were not very fussed about upsetting the relative peace. The most public attempt at rapprochement was in 1965 by Pat Kennelly, the ALP Deputy Leader in the Senate, but it failed. Whitlam's Deputy, Lance Barnard, also began talks on Whitlam's behalf in 1968, but without success. Not only was the union Left an insuperable obstacle, but after the years of mutual vitriol the respective members and supporters would have been difficult to merge. And few were willing to give up real or hoped-for parliamentary positions to make way for DLP people.

Mannix's successor, Archbishop Justin Simonds shared the 'Sydney line' of disapproval of a free run for Santamaria and set out to ease the acrimonious, divisive and politicised atmosphere of the Melbourne Archdiocese. The climate had been such that some senior clergy were advising that to vote Labor was sinful, because of its links with communism. Simonds removed Santamaria as a commentator for the official Catholic TV program, cracked down on politics from the pulpit and banned the sale of *News Weekly* on church property. The DLP vote did not diminish, however. Half the Catholics in Victoria still were still determined to protest against the controllers of the ALP. Jim Brosnan, who became Federal President of the DLP, used to joke, of Calwell, Chamberlain and other ALP controllers, 'They've never let us down yet.'

Santamaria got a new, national and more influential platform as a TV commentator with his 'Point of View' segment on media tycoon Frank Packer's Channel 9 and also from 1976 a column in *The Australian*. Jack Kane's rapport with Frank Packer was useful in arranging the Channel 9 spot. Santamaria became one of the country's best known commentators. On TV, in his distinctively emphatic and deliberate enunciation, he was quick to point to examples of the 'pro-communist left' at work in the ALP, especially in his priority, defence and foreign policy. In *The Australian* he embraced social and religious conservatism, and opposition to deregulation and free trade, in a graceful, often witty way, unlike his strident side. His sharp pen deflated alike libertarians, theologians and bankers, feminists, football administrators and free traders. He could sound like an old man weeping for the past, but perhaps his causes were not so much unpopular as unfashionable.

Labor failed dismally at the 1966 election, with a national vote down to 40 per cent. This was largely due to Calwell's faltering leadership, his age showing, his rhetoric painful, his policies patently impractical, his seizing on the war in Vietnam coarsely opportunistic, his dependence on the organisational wing increasingly widely understood. He finally stood down for Whitlam at the beginning of 1967.

Whitlam's strategy was of necessity to try to make the existing party more electable. With rapprochement with the DLP unlikely, his aim was to appeal to the voters themselves, whether DLP or coalition, and win over enough to take Labor's vote up to 51 per cent. He was easily at home with the new TV era, the best performer of his kind at the time, greyingly distinguished in appearance, fluent, polished, quick and witty. He was also the best parliamentary and public orator since Menzies, helped by the distinctive crafting of his serendipitous speech-writer Graham Freudenberg. Together they offered some great lines that cut through to people. Whitlam used public appearances to press for party reform, appealing to the membership and public over the heads of the organisation, and emphasising his and his team's relative independence of the 'machine', left or right.

Whitlam was not at first always popular internally. His family background and personal style was distinctly middle-class; he was the Canberra-raised son of a former Commonwealth Solicitor-General. A little stiff at first meeting, he was a non-practicing Protestant, lived in the Sydney outer suburbs, had not taken much interest in internal party politics, and could at times be brusque and tactless in manner and seem arrogant and egocentric. It was not forgotten that he had been on the platform for Evatt's alarmist speech at Port Kembla in 1955. In short, he was not a natural fit with the NSW Right, and even less a natural fit interstate. The Left often called him the 'Labor Menzies'. In his fight for internal change, he spoke famously of the Federal Executive as 'twelve witless men'. He ridiculed as vacuous the Left's claims that it was preserving party 'principles' and said of the line that change would put these principles at stake, 'only the impotent are pure'.

But his commitment and willingness to take risks, his enthusiasm for winning office and for what a national Labor Government could do for the country (and for many individuals) and his sheer talent gradually won friends, at first on the Right and then grudgingly some on the Left. With the NSW Right behind him, Whitlam's pre-selection was secure. He also won over voters. The election of October 1969, when the coalition leadership of John Gorton was failing, saw Labor surge to 47 per cent of the vote. By then too, not only was the coalition struggling internally, but the Vietnam War was at its peak and biting unpredictably as a political issue. This doubled with conscription of 20-year-olds for overseas army service, which had been introduced in the Indonesia-Malaysia crisis of 1964. The huge inflow of young 'baby boom' voters came at about the same time, typically an anti-war vote. Whitlam opposed the war and conscription, but more subtly and gently than the harshly anti-American Left and Calwell. The Vietnam issue and the soaring youth vote at a time of exceptionable social change also threatened a DLP vote already owing signs of weakness.

Whitlam's biggest problem lay in Victoria, where the DLP vote remained strong, the left-wing ALP controllers obdurate and the Labor vote struggled at around 40 per cent or less. The Victorian ALP had been the Communist Party's main toehold. In the first decade after the Split, the Communist Party relied on as go-between its affable and personally popular Trades Hall operator, George Seelaf of the Meat Workers' union. Seelaf had a good sense of how far to push his Party's ambitions for a united front and dealt in the ALP with Don McSween of the Clothing Trades, an old-style far left apparatchik. By the mid-60s, as the influence of these two waned, the situation can only be described as convoluted.

When Stout died in 1964, his Assistant Secretary at the Trades Hall Council, Mick Jordan, won a bitterly contested election against the Left's Jack Wood for the position of Secretary. The Left loathed Jordan, an old-time union moderate who had helped organise the grouper takeover of the State ALP in 1950 – ironically, then as Stout's man. Jordan retained a visceral inclination to stand up to overbearing communist union officials, stemming back to his origins in the necessarily moderate Textile union. His election broke up the cosy arrangement of Stout's later days. Because of the differing electoral systems, Jordan's win did not translate into the ALP Conference, but it unsettled the Left.

One of the architects of Jordan's victory was the future Senate Leader John Button, then a 31-year-old union lawyer with the Maurice Blackburn firm. Such was the Trades Hall paranoia about the NCC/DLP and other critics that Button and the NCC National Industrial Officer, John Maynes (who was also Federal President of the Clerks' Union) met in a park to arrange a joint effort. Button next organised sympathetic branch members into a reform body, known as 'The Participants' in order to avoid the tainted word 'group'. These worked with Jordan's unions and Whitlam to campaign for change and together could get a third of the votes at State Conference. They campaigned for a more open, representative organisation and more say for branches and parliamentarians. Under the post-1955 administration, the local branch structure had declined, while pre-selection by a notoriously suspicious, vindictive executive made for apathetic politicians. The State Parliamentary Party was deliberately kept ineffectual and shared the abysmal Labor vote of Commonwealth elections, at around 37-38 per cent.

The late 60s also brought much – and unpredictable – competitive jostling for influence in the evolving Melbourne Trades Hall Left. The Communist Party Split into 'pro-Moscow' and 'pro-Peking' parties (the 'caviars' and 'dim sims') and then a mainstream, more moderate, independent Communist Party. The Vietnam era turmoil threw up Trotskyist and 'New Left' groupings – and there were even those with suspected links to the Soviet KGB, Iraq and Cuba. There were also union officials crafting a genuine ALP Left position for the new circumstances. Nearly all, though, had a low priority, if not disdain, for parliamentary government. The State Secretary from 1963, Bill Hartley, was a Chamberlain protégé from Perth whose allegiance in the new conditions was uncertain.

By 1970 the scent of victory had brought most of the party behind Whitlam, except for Chamberlain and the Victorians. It was becoming a bitterly personal Chamberlain versus Whitlam battle. Whitlam sensationally attracted a crucial ally in Clyde Cameron, the Adelaide MP who had earlier run Ward's campaign for the leadership and was one of those who drove the Split. Whitlam convinced Cameron that he (Cameron) could now be more effective in government than out and promised to make him Minister for Labor. Cameron then used his dominant influence to bring the South Australian branch of the Party, which held the balance of power federally, over to Whitlam. It was also, from a South Australian viewpoint, a favourable time in the State electoral timetable to risk turbulence in the wider Party, with Premier Don Dunstan's government enjoying mid-term popularity and prestige.

In a drawn-out drama Cameron, stockily built ex-shearer and bush intellectual, charming, devious and a good hater, broke with Chamberlain, teamed up with the NSW Right and brought the same shrewd, ruthless tactical skills he had used fifteen years earlier to secure a Federal Executive intervention that sacked the Victorian Executive and reorganised the state branch. To make this more palatable, the Federal Executive also intervened in NSW to broaden the administrative structure – without seriously weakening the NSW Right. Under the hapless Hartley, the Victorians had been too stubborn by half over State Aid in the 1970 State election and stumbled erratically when Cameron attacked. Labor's dog days were over and on 2 December 1972 Australia made Edward Gough Whitlam Prime Minister.

Chapter 8

After Half a Century

'Santamaria' and 'Split' issues continued to be part of Australian politics and government into the Twenty-first Century though receding to the margins. Labor's win under Gough Whitlam in 1972 critically wounded the Democratic Labor Party, since its years-old strategy of keeping the ALP out office pending a rapprochement had failed. However, it still controlled the balance of power in the Senate and with the coalition blocked several measures for which Labor claimed a popular mandate. The coalition also threatened to block money supply. The DLP had chosen the Victorian Frank McManus as Parliamentary Leader ahead of Vincent Gair, the former ALP Premier of Queensland, after the 1972 election. Angry at frequent Senate obstruction, Whitlam in 1974 offered the unhappy Gair the post of Australian Ambassador to Ireland. Gair accepted and resigned from the Senate. This new 'Gair Affair' outraged the DLP, which looked on it as defection.

Whitlam then secured, and narrowly won, a Double Dissolution of the Parliament and all five DLP senators were defeated, the Party's standing tarnished by Gair. A Joint Sitting of both houses passed contested Labor legislation, including that for Medibank, fore-runner of Medicare, but the DLP was left with nowhere to go. All its senators were gone, its vote was plummeting and the old issues were fading, with the Communist Party itself in similar trouble; neither had much appeal to a new generation influenced by the liberalising spirit of the day and buoyant capitalism. In 1978 the DLP voted to disband; it did not want to become a 'backyard operation', as one official put it, but a 'rump' Party of enthusiasts continued and could occasionally win a minor vote.

The former DLP vote was estimated to have split about evenly between the main parties, but also to have further enlarged the growing pool of swinging voters. The 'Catholic vote' in as far as it was distinguishable, was now reckoned to be evenly spread between both sides of politics. NCC members and sympathisers often joined the Liberal or National parties, whereas before 1955 they usually joined the ALP. Within the coalition they were a force for social conservatism, but cautioun about the deregulationist and free market and free trade approach of the times.

The main Communist Party also voted itself out of existence in 1991. It had become all too clear that neither Moscow nor Peking had anything to offer Australia and the two big communist powers themselves were moderating fast in the 1970s, although the brief period of socialist drama on university campuses gave aspiring revolutionaries short-lived hope. A 'pro-Moscow' splinter, at first called the 'Socialist Party of Australia' (SPA), continued into the new century and took up the Communist Party name after the main party disbanded, but its numbers were tiny and members mostly elderly. A 'Maoist' Party had also hived off, but fizzled out after a brief period of spark in the university campus disruptions around 1970. Again, the problem was that capitalism had all too clearly won.

The National Civic Council supported the disbandment of the DLP, but itself continued active. It had influence or control in several older unions and carved out new territory in the burgeoning white-collar field. Like the communists it also moved to the right, but increasingly in the sense of moving closer to the Liberals. NCC industrial operators were no longer especially controversial, other than sometimes for conservative policies and because they tended to be secretive about their allegiance.

It was instructive that Santamaria formed a close personal friendship with Menzies, until Menzies died in 1978. Over a whisky or two, they became soul mates sad about the passing of an older, more secure and predictable Australia with more orderly values than the freer-flowing society that emerged in the 1970s. Santamaria also enjoyed a good relationship with Malcolm Fraser, the Liberal Prime Minister from 1975–83, who as Opposition Leader denied supply to Whitlam in 1975, leading to the historic 'dismissal' of Whitlam.

Santamaria had also through the DLP influenced earlier post-Split Liberal governments in favour of strong defence, social conservatism and State Aid for independent schools and contributed to the downfall of Prime Minister John Gorton in 1971.

Santamaria increasingly devoted more NCC energy and resources away from the unions towards 'social' questions, such as student politics, universities more generally and issues like abortion, euthanasia and maintaining the primacy of the conventional family. This brought him and the NCC closer to Protestant, Jewish and other social conservatives. The NCC adopted the old communist strategy of 'fronts', groups which it started and encouraged on particular issues, where it could attract non-members principally concerned about the issue involved. This strategy could also be seen (in the non-profit sense) as Santamaria acting like a shrewd, typically autocratic small businessman, cultivating new markets for his firm as older ones weakened. These bodies included the Defend Australia Committee, The Australian Defence Association, university Democratic Clubs, The Australian Council for Educational Standards, Campion Books, Peace with Freedom, The Australian Family Association, Women Who Want to Be Women, Thomas More Centre and the Council for the National Interest. The effectiveness and degree of NCC involvement varied.

The Church itself also took up much effort. He had deep reservations about developments in the Catholic Church after the Vatican 11 Council of the mid-60s. He argued that it was not so much the letter of the Council's resolutions but the way they were being interpreted. The NCC became a vehicle for the conservative wing of Catholicism, as against the various more liberal strands that followed the Council. These related to doctrine, discipline and a liberalising or left-wing bent on particular issues. Catholicism became a much more diverse, 'broad', less 'triumphal' church than the one Santamaria had begun to serve half a century earlier. Whether or not this led to a big decline in attendance at Mass, as Santamaria claimed, was unknowable. The NCC published the religious magazine *AD2000* to promote the conservative view.

The 'liberal' Catholic spirit developed in much the same way and same time as the Protestant ecumenical movement, which also sought to lower barriers between the various churches, re-examine old doctrines – including the understanding and context of the Bible – and encourage Christian unity. These ideas had been spreading quietly among those interested since the 1920s, but gathered pace in the '50s and by the 1960s were rapidly changing – some would day belatedly modernising – worldwide Christendom as a whole. In the new atmosphere, the old 'sectarian' feeling, with its suspicions and resentments, faded in Australia.

Santamaria's greatest success in an adult lifetime of trying with varied success to influence politicians was Tony Abbott, who became Prime Minister in 2013, though long after the old man's death. (An internal rebellion in the parliamentary Liberal Party voted Abbott out of the leadership in 2015, but this was nothing to do with his admiration for Santamaria.) Abbott was an assertive, ebullient force of nature in Sydney University politics as a leader of the Democratic Club. Unlike other politicians, he was markedly open about his admiration for Santamaria. Democratic Clubs were an NCC initiative to organise against the campus left. For several years they allied with both Labor and Liberal student organisations to successfully oppose the 'hard left' controllers of the National Union of Australian University Students. The campus left was then, after the more excitable phase a few years earlier, extreme and unattractive, suspected of rather lavishly using student funds. As usual with student politics, this phase ended as students departed and the Democratic Clubs wilted for lack of a cause. 'Left' causes continued to rise and fall on campus. A left-wing atmosphere was common but it was vague, amorphous and 'politically correct', varying from militant Marxism through to the conventional centre politics, without any clear division. Unlike in the old days of the Communist Party, there was not much solid organisation left to attack. The NCC also set up, but with limited success, Peace with Freedom, to counter the neutralist tendency among academics on foreign affairs.

The turn of emphasis away from the unions led to the NCC itself splitting. The industrial organisers found themselves more and more a separate and seemingly lower status section, with a reduced share of the money and effort. As Santamaria, like a lot of other people, became more conservative as he grew older, he became a critic of the trade unions in general and their impact on the society. With the fight against communism over, the industrial section was preoccupied with everyday industrial relations issues, which held little interest for Santamaria. The industrialists frequently disagreed with him, deplored his 'tin ear' for the Labor Movement and also thought he was keeping the overseas trips, meetings with interesting people and the like to for himself. Personality and policy clashes worsened and a separate faction developed under the National Industrial Officer and Movement veteran, John Maynes, who was also National President of the Federated Clerks' Union, an NCC stronghold. A struggle for control developed and the industrialists bitterly and sadly formed the impression that Santamaria was trying to drive them out to maintain the control that was slipping away from him towards Maynes. Some had worked with Santamaria for a generation or more and been the mainstay of the supposed *raison d'être*, in the unions. Santamaria had previously volunteered in 1979 to retire the following year at 65, but colleagues pressed him to stay. He showed no further sign of retiring. Now it was as if, like a generation earlier, another old man was hanging on too long and too rigidly, unwilling to give up his power. The manoeuvring that followed was reminiscent of the Split of thirty years before. It ended in 1983 with dismissal of major NCC figures of many years standing and the resignation of others. The pre-breach National Secretary of the NCC, Gerald Mercer, Maynes and the other industrial organisers, together with supporters, formed a separate organisation, Social Action, later the Industrial Action Fund, much more based in the union offices. Many were regarded as good union officials.

Several former 'grouper' unions had disaffiliated from the Victorian ALP in 1955 and though not formally affiliated to the DLP did not re-join the ALP when it moderated after the 1970 intervention or when the DLP and Communist Party collapsed. Ties with the NCC had varied, but they tended to work as a bloc. They were not especially keen to reaffiliate and there was still substantial opposition to them in the ALP, but the breach with Santamaria eased the situation. Bob Hawke, President of ACTU 1969–80, wanted to strengthen moderate elements when he became Prime Minister in 1983, and brokered a deal for rapprochement. The four 'grouper' unions took their places at the 1984 Victorian Conference, to be greeted by flying rotten tomatoes from Socialist Left rowdies. But melodrama aside, after thirty years the Split was finally over.

The returning unions were the Clerks, Ironworkers, Shop Assistants and Carpenters and Joiners.

Like the rest of the union movement, their fortunes over the next years varied. The fast decline of Australian manufacturing with globalisation at the same time as a rapid turn to automation and small contractors, especially in the 1990s, brought a huge fall in the blue collar workforce and thus union membership. The unions turned to amalgamations – on a scale some thought excessive – to survive and to more integration with the white-collar bodies. The amalgamations saw the Federated Ironworkers' Association, scene of the most dramatic battle of the Cold War, merge with its one-time enemy, the Australian Workers' Union. The Clerks, bastion of the Right, fell to a well organised takeover from the Left.

The 'shoppies', now the Shop, Distributive & Allied Employees Association, became the nucleus of a socially conservative force in the ALP, with some policies Santamaria would have approved. But the main controversy was just that some people disagreed with these policies; the awe of old was gone. Parliamentarians often welcomed the SDA as a counter to the pressure for fast social change from the Left. Even Julia Gillard, notionally a left-wing feminist, expressed gratitude in her memoirs for support from Joe de Bruyn, the union's National President. The 'shoppies' nevertheless could be seen as grandchildren of Santamaria and the Movement.

By this time the bigger, but fewer unions – with a much smaller proportion of the population as members – looked more like middle-sized corporate or government bureaucracies than the small, specialist unions of the past, with their austere little offices in drafty old trades halls and often closeness to the manual worker members. Many, if not most, of their officials and employees had tertiary education and the new 'super unions', often with superannuation links, had big budgets and roomy, stylish modern offices.

The long periods out of office, and thus inexperience, after the Split affected Labor in its first post-Split governments. The Whitlam Government from 1972–75, the first Labor Government since 1949, did not live up to the grandiose promise surrounding it. It tried to do too much too quickly, some of it of dubious worth, and ran into serious budgetary difficulty. A big part of its many problems was that no minister or back-bencher had ever been an MP, let alone a minister, during a Labor Government. It lacked the sense of pace and discipline of many effective state Labor governments, let alone conservative ones. Labor people other than Whitlam had given little thought during the long years in opposition as to how Labor would handle government. Whitlam's many policies were clear, but they had never been much analysed and often reflected his Canberra youth, when Federal Government was still under-developed. They envisaged a huge expansion of government and shift in power to the Commonwealth. He also envisaged continued prosperity, with its rising tax yield, at the level of the late 1960s. The economy was to prove uncooperative, but also Whitlam's uncritical plans for bigger government came just as the world was turning away from the government expansion trend that had prevailed since the 1930s Forty years later Whitlam's vision would have been regarded as misguidedly excessive and likely to cost too much, clog up the works and achieve little.

Labor came to office in Victoria in 1982, for the first time since the Split in 1955. The Premier was John Cain Junior, son of the namesake 1955 Premier. Even after the lessons of the Whitlam era, it tried to do too much, not all worth it, and got into enough serious debt and public odium, to be ignominiously ousted in 1990 when Victoria turned to the free marketing new rightist Jeff Kennett.

Junior people in both governments quietly learned the lessons, however. The Federal Labor government led by Bob Hawke (1983–91) and Paul Keating (1991–96) paid much more attention to good process, watching the budget and taking the people with it. Later Victorian governments also moved cautiously and were generally successful. The Hawke Government was the first to frankly disown the old 'class war' with its hankering for public ownership and 'tax and spend' ways and instead worked with business to enlarge the national 'cake'. Hawke and more so his deputy, Paul Keating, lived lavishly, dressed stylishly and mixed conspicuously with the very rich – the more raffish of whom they probably wished later they had not. 'Socialism' had receded to the margins of the left wing, where it had to jostle for attention with feminism, environmentalism and many other causes. These were among the causes the Labor governments of Kevin Rudd and Julia Gillard (2007–13) had to juggle, along with the dominant moderate views of middle Australia.

Labor did not return to office in Queensland until 1989, under Premier Wayne Goss.

B.A. Santamaria died on 25 February 1998 of a brain tumour, aged 82, in office as President of the NCC until the end, prevented by his last illness from giving a planned speech in Adelaide and his first meeting with an architect of the Split, Clyde Cameron, by then a mellower retired MP in his mid-80s, attracted to the NCC's hostile views on the free market. More than two-thousand mourners overflowed from St Patrick's Cathedral in East Melbourne for Santamaria's funeral. The celebrant was the Archbishop of Melbourne, George Pell. The Prime Minister of Australia, John Howard had visited he death bed and was a notable mourner at the funeral.

Chapter 9

Memory Lane

Greener in the ways of life than I thought I was when in the mid-60s I first started interviewing for the original *Split*, I asked DLP senator Frank McManus how much the groupers had been influenced by the Papal Social Encyclicals, as commentators had often reported. 'Most of them would want to know what race it started in,' the fatherly but usually dour senator replied.

Anger entered his voice as he added, 'It wasn't ideological, it was a power struggle'. He then explained the intricacies of Melbourne Trades Hall internal politics in the 1950s, which – like their interstate counterparts – were somewhat less elevated than people seemed to be believing a decade on. It could be classed as industrial Labor versus the political wing, but again this gives it a lofty, political science flavour. There was an element of that, but its force came from the bitterness of individual union elections – that is, elections over the careers and livelihood of officials – control of 3KZ, the Trades Hall-owned radio station and some very bitter personality clashes. And there was more. For example, the arcane industrial politics of the Latrobe Valley.

I asked McManus about the role of Bob Santamaria, but he brushed the question aside awkwardly, except to suggest irritatedly that Santamaria could argue too well for comfort and the result was often not for the best.

I asked about Stan Keon and Jack Mullins, the Labor parliamentarians most associated in the public mind with the Movement, Split and rise of the DLP. 'They stirred it up in the first place and then wouldn't stick with us,' he said sourly, a sentiment others would also express.

With his good memory, straightforwardness and orderly, school teacher's mind, McManus was one of the few intimately involved in the Split who actually seemed to understand and be able to cogently explain the full picture. Most people I spoke to seemed concerned mainly with the limited part they knew about or played themselves.

I was also mildly surprised – at first – to find how much politicians thought like sales managers on big questions of public policy, as products that might or might not 'go' with the public, rather than as issues in themselves, as most voters would expect. Politicians need to have big egos and learn to think and speak strategically or they are ineffective. Their public 'image' is necessarily superficial; the real people can be more interesting.

The most revealing discovery to me was how little most people involved thought about ideology. There seemed enough of it in the background of both the DLP/NCC and the trades halls to attract half the world's universities: Catholic social theory and church authority on one hand, variations of Marxism, social democracy and other socialism on the other. But ideology hardly arose at all in the innumerable interviews and informal conversations I had; and if it did was usually in the context of being dismissed as unimportant. The politics at hand was the game.

DLP people were the most reflective of those I interviewed, as one might expect of the losing side. ALP people usually seemed to have the satisfaction of winners, but with that characteristic stubborn party loyalty they rarely looked far into the intricacies. A decade on, many believed the Split had been a necessary, if searing experience to remove a noxious virus that had all but taken over the party. Their chief objection to the DLP though was that it for so long and so loudly insulted their party in public and kept it from office.

The winners had been writing the history. The losers, when they wrote at all, showed mainly indignation that it that it could have happened when they were doing such a good job, with groupers beating 'the comms' in the unions and building up ALP strength in numbers and votes. They were often amenable to perceiving conspiracies, again by 'the comms' or by 'anti-Catholics', along with the detested but incomprehensible Dr Evatt. Many of those involved had a poor understanding of the interstate politics. One New South Wales senator said he had not understood it all properly until he read my book.

After McManus I secured an interview – or thought I had – with Stan Keon, the parliamentarian most associated with the DLP side in the Split years. He had lost his seat in 1955 to future Deputy Prime Minister Jim Cairns. Keon invited me to join him for lunch at his favourite haunt, the Café Latin, in Lonsdale Street, Melbourne, where he once had often lunched with Santamaria and other grouper MPs. He was sitting at a table with several friends and introduced me, but no opportunity for questions or discussion of the past arose. I decided that he didn't like answering questions and was messing me round. But as we walked down the street afterwards he let some snippets go: 'I thought the Movement were a lot of boy scouts'; and 'It (the Grouper/Movement complex) was not big enough for both of us'. (Santamaria and himself.)

I ran into him socially a few times over the years after the book was published and he was friendly and often released more snippets. 'You hardly mentioned me', he complained the first time we met again. (It was not true.) Later he recalled that once in the small hours when he was in a deep sleep after a hard time in Canberra, Evatt rang him when he saw the morning papers. 'You're my friend. Why are you attacking me?' the embattled but confused Opposition Leader complained. 'Because you're attacking me', Stan sleepily replied. 'But it's not you I'm attacking,' a perplexed Evatt said, 'I'm attacking Santamaria.' Another time Keon said awkwardly that some of his shriller statements in parliament had been in part due to staying too long in the Members' bar.

Witty to a fault and affable, Keon seemed to me a natural politician, deeply hurt by the Split even though he had become a prosperous wine merchant. There might have been a touch of embarrassment that he had not been a good enough politician to save his side. But, though admittedly on slight acquaintance, I saw little of the strident, obsessive anti-communist and Catholic puritan he presented as in his earlier days. He did let it slip once, though, in the 1980s – long before New York's 9/11 – that he felt psychologically threatened by the Muslims. Once he left politics, he seems to have just lost interest in the issues the Movement promoted and he had once so passionately advocated.

McManus seemed to be what he had always been, a mix of old-style Labor (his father was a union official), conservative Catholic and intense anti-communist. Once in the 1970s when Russian naval units began sailing into the Indian Ocean, he urged that Australia form an alliance with South Africa – in the dying days of apartheid – against them.

I found Bob Santamaria polite, fluent, helpful and less evasive than many, but neither as spell-binding and charismatic nor as central to events as I and others expected. I got the impression – as with Keon – that he felt both dreadfully hurt by the Split and the personal tirades and vilification that followed but also chastened and embarrassed by some of his own hubris and excesses then. He seemed to struggle with his ego. He had the knack of making a fairly routine statement, for example, 'I take notice of what men do, not what they say' sound wise and authoritative. He also blamed a pervasive anti-Catholicism for almost everything that had gone wrong. 'We would have had a better Australia than we have now,' he said of the Movement's many 'positive policies' that were never implemented and had mostly invited either scorn or apathy. For better or worse, I never had the opportunity to hear him in full oratorical flight to a sympathetic audience.

I came to agree with others that he was better at what he was against than what he was for, a bit theoretical and intellectual and just not a 'Labor man' in that instinctive, distinctive way a good Labor politician (and some of his colleagues) were. He had never been to a State ALP Conference, some who were otherwise sympathetic, complained and it showed. My overall feeling was that people he worked with usually liked him personally, respected his strength as a leader and supported the main thrust of Movement/NCC work. But they often felt exasperated by his patchy judgment and controlling tendencies and suspected a touch of narcissism. Others almost revered his clarity of mind, charisma, eloquence and commitment. It was not unlike a lot of other politics, including office politics. He also seemed at times to have a fellow feeling for the communists, as ideologically pure, worthy enemies, if wrong. He was impatient with the messiness of mainstream politics.

He never seemed to quite grasp that highly organised influencing or control by one organisation in the affairs of another could be counter-productive – in my observation human nature doesn't like it unless in very strong agreement with the 'outside organisation'.

Santamaria did know a lot about the events, though and willingly – and persuasively – answered my questions reasonably openly. I decided that he was not a bad bloke, but yet another control freak; I certainly wouldn't want to be on the wrong side of him in the National Civic Council.

Bob Holt, Victorian President of the ALP in the mid-60s and a former minister in the State Labor Government that was destroyed in 1955, welcomed me warmly and seemed open, but became tongue-tied when I pressed him on sensitive points, such as his charge that Santamaria had threatened his pre-selection when denied Crown land for a farming scheme. Santamaria as vehemently denied that charge and Holt fobbed me off for a follow-up interview, even by phone. Later I found that he had a reputation on both sides as erratic under pressure, though in the '60s he became a 'pretty face' moderate token president for the Party's most left-wing state branch.

Pat Kennelly, then Deputy ALP Leader in the Senate, was another who was initially charming but became uneasy even with polite questioning that was actually still fairly naïve. Denis Lovegrove, then Victorian Deputy Leader of the Opposition but State Secretary from 1950, was uneasy too, but without the initial charm. Awkwardly, he said that his grouper former colleagues had been mistaken and bound to lose by breaking away from the ALP. Mick Jordan, by then Secretary of the Trades Hall Council, agreed.

Arthur Calwell, the Opposition Leader, made the very Calwellian quip about Dr Evatt, 'At first I thought he was bad but now I think he was mad.' He had also mistrusted Santamaria since the 1940s.

Clyde Cameron was ever proud of being 'numbers man' for the drive to create a nationalising, defence isolationist left-wing party. I once happened on him waiting near Calwell's office in tears soon after his hero Eddie Ward died; I was going to have a beer with Calwell's press secretary, Graham Freudenberg. Years later I had several talks with Cameron.

John Ducker, Yorkshire-born 'bruvver' of the industrial wing right in Sydney a generation later, complained about not being mentioned at all in the original book. I didn't like to tell him that the reason was that, as an Ironworkers' union organiser in his early 20s at the time, he was not important enough. Frank Rooney was put out that I didn't interview him. I should have, but time away from home was always limited.

Laurie Short, General Secretary of the Ironworkers for thirty-four years after the Industrial Groups win in 1952, was another who was clear, crisp and direct in interviews. He must have liked the result, because years later he commissioned me (with Kate White) to write a 70th anniversary history of the union, the Federated Ironworkers' Association of Australia.

The DLP office in Melbourne held the official pre-Split records of the Victorian branch of the ALP, pending the reconciliation that never came, and the officers made them freely available. I was grateful for the cups of tea, but also struck up personally as well as professionally good friendships with Jim Brosnan, the Party's Federal President and John Foley, the state organiser. In ALP eyes at the time, I would have been risking contagion by being there at all. Nevertheless, I had a couple of agreeable evenings in the Kilkenny Inn with the DLP State executive after their meetings.

One of my earliest recollections of these events was riding my bike to Hampton High School in suburban Melbourne, past a postwar Housing Commission building site, where pro and anti-communist union leaflets were lying about. Some other early memories: The drama when, as a copy boy for *The Argus* newspaper in Melbourne, the scandalous Cold War novel *Power Without Glory* first appeared in 1950. *The Argus* was unwittingly involved in mechanically cutting the printed sheets to page size, as a contract printing job but wild rumours spread about communist involvement and it earned a shrill attack in Parliament from Stan Keon. *Power Without Glory* was important in building up the psychological climate for the Split. Another memory from that time is chatting with the paper's colourful Labor writer Jack O'Sullivan, allegedly an ally of Pat Kennelly, about Catholic Action – by then all the buzz in the rumour mill – allegedly taking over the Victorian ALP, with McManus its head man. The bigger move at that time, though, was that this factional shift was in short-lived alliance with the industrial wing headed by Vic Stout and Mick Jordan of the Trades Hall Council. All were to continue as players in the dramas to come, though sides changed.

The daily and periodical press, which I trust I used shrewdly, was the best source of all. Daily reports, when read consecutively and along with other information, give a much sounder impression than if read scrappily day to day. The innumerable news and feature items had a mixture of reports of quotations from official statements and participants' comments, 'leaks' and 'insider' material. It was mostly, but not always, reliable and not often badly biassed. One weakness was that the Canberra correspondents did not always understand the intricacies of local trades hall politics – and the trades hall reporters could be weak on the Canberra implications.

Alan Reid was the most notable of many contemporary journalists writing in the Split years and a help to me. The Falstaffian Ian Fitchett, chief political writer for *The Age* and later *Sydney Morning Herald*, was especially helpful through his day to day reporting on events. It had the whiff of backgrounding by the 'Pro-Evatt' side, but seemed always thorough and reliable. Fitchett's crucial reports appeared in *The Age* in November 1954 saying that the Federal Executive, which Evatt had called in, could not find evidence, despite long hearings, to support Evatt's charge that Santamaria and the Movement controlled the Victorian branch. But the 'Feds' decided to take it over anyway because the politics of not doing so were too difficult.

Another pressman with a role I only discovered later, was Hal Myers, the *Sydney Morning Herald* correspondent at the time, who in addition to being a good all-round reporter, had Bill Bourke, the Victorian MP who went briefly, to the DLP side, as a 'leak' and they became good personal friends. Evatt suspected this and thought, incorrectly, that Bourke, who he had until then been cultivating, was leaking on behalf of the Santamaria plot. I interviewed Bourke and liked him, but he did not reveal this then other than to recommend Myers' reporting to me. Only forty-five years later did Myers reveal the connection in his autobiography, *The Whispering Gallery* (Kangaroo Press 1999).

Bourke told me though that at the Monday 'grouper' lunches at the Latin, his impression was that Keon was trying to influence (or he might have said manipulate) Santamaria and vice-versa. But he thought Santamaria had the edge. Bourke seemed to be a fair-minded lawyer in a borderline seat who over-reacted not only to Evatt's extravagances in promising to abolish the means test on age pensions and then over the Petrov affair, but ironically also over Evatt's pre-Split cultivation of Santamaria and the resulting Church involvement. He acknowledged that he was not a great natural politician. According to McManus, Bourke had used the Movement to get pre-selection and then 'put on a white shirt' to distance himself from it.

A pressman with an interesting background was Kevin Power, Canberra Correspondent for the Sydney *Daily Mirror.* He was a cousin of Helen Santamaria, Bob's first wife and his reports sometimes hinted at this. The left wing of the Canberra Press Gallery thought him somewhat suspect.

The Sydney Trades Hall reporters could be a rum lot and I enjoyed their salty pub yarning: Fred Coleman-Brown, Keith Martin, Jack Simpson among them. And there was the Sydney landlady Mrs Wilkinson, who beamed over breakfast that 'Eddie (Ward) was givin' it to old Bob (Menzies)' in parliament on the radio the night before.

Yarning over the years with politically astute old mates helped us all sort some of the story in our own minds. Kevin Hilferty, Graham Freudenberg, Dick Hall, Tony Coady and Brian Buckley especially come to mind. Informal discussions with dozens of people complemented about twenty interviews.

Many more helped than can be mentioned in this memoir. Nearly all the people, mentioned or not, have passed on now, but all were memorable in their way and much appreciated.

Nobody will believe that writers on politics are not biased. I have tried not to be. I was a member of the ALP in Victoria from 1964–70, at first out of innocent interest about how it worked, but soon was quite involved as volunteer editor of *Labor Comment*, a miniscule monthly put out by the somewhat clandestine group known as 'The Participants' to campaign for change in the Victorian branch of the Party. We soon realised what an ineffectual, bullying and unlovely mess the Split had left. I realised too that I was not by temperament a political party animal and let my membership lapse after the 1970 intervention.

Bibliography

Albinski, H.S., *Australian Politics and Attitudes Towards China*, Princeton University Press, 1965

Bray, Mark and Rimmer, Malcolm, *Carrying the Goods, A History of The Transport Workers Union, 1888–1986*, Allen and Unwin, Sydney, 1987

Brennan, Nile, *Dr Mannix*, Rigby, Adelaide, 1964

Chamberlain, F.E., *A Selection of Talks and Articles*, Western Australian branch of the ALP, 1964

Costar, Brian, Love, Peter and Strangio, Paul (eds.), *The Great Labor Schism*, Scribe, Melbourne, 2005

Crisp, L.F., *Ben Chifley, a Biography*, Longmans, Melbourne, 1960

Dalziel, Alan, *Evatt - the Enigma*, Lansdowne Press, Melbourne, 1967

Duffy, Paul, Catholic Judgments on the origins and growth of the ALP Dispute 1954–61, unpublished thesis in Melbourne University Library, 1968

Duncan, Bruce, *Crusade or Conspiracy, Catholics and the Anti-Communist Struggle in Australia*, Sydney, 2001

Freudenberg, Graham, *A Certain Grandeur, Gough Whitlam in Politics*, Macmillan, Melbourne, 1977

Gillard, Julia, *My Story*, Random House, 2014

Griffin, James, *Daniel Mannix, Beyond the Myths*, Garratt, Melbourne, 2012

Henderson, Gerard, *Santamaria, A Most Unusual Man*, Melbourne, 2015

Lack, Clem (ed.), *Three Decades of Queensland Political History, 1929–60*, Queensland Government Printer, Brisbane, 1962

Morgan, Patrick, *B.A. Santamaria, Your Most Obedient Servant, Selected Letters*, Melbourne, 2007

Morgan, Patrick, *B.A. Santamaria, Running the Show, Selected Documents*, Melbourne, 2008

Murray, Robert, *The Split, Australian Labor in The Fifties,* Melbourne, 1970

Murray, Robert with Kate White, *The Ironworkers: A History of the Federated Ironworkers' Association of Australia*, Sydney, 1983

Niall, Brenda, *Mannix*, Text, 2015

O'Farrell, P.J., *The Catholic Church in Australia*, Nelson, Melbourne, 1968

Ormonde, Paul (ed.), *Santamaria: The Politics of Fear,* Spectrum, Melbourne, 2000

Peoples, Kevin, *Santamaria's Salesman,* Garrratt, Melbourne, 2012

Santamaria, B.A., *Against The Tide*, Melbourne, 1981

Santamaria, B.A., *Daniel Mannix, A Biography,* Melbourne, 1984

Index

Printed in Australia
AUOC02n0724090317
283707AU00004B/4/P

9 781925 333596